Outwitting the Job Market

Everything You Need to Locate and Land a Great Position

Series Concept Created by Bill Adler, Jr.

THE LYONS PRESS

Guilford, Connecticut

An imprint of The Globe Pequot Press

OUTWITTING™ is a trademark of Adler and Robin Books, Inc., and is licensed to The Lyons Press, Inc., and its permitted licensees for use with this series. The concept for the series was created by Bill Adler, Jr.

The Lyons Press is an imprint of The Globe Pequot Press.

10 9 8 7 6 5 4 3 2 1

Printed in the United States of America

Designed by Stephanie Doyle

ISBN 1-59228-350-0

Library of Congress Cataloging-in-Publication Data is available on file.

This book is for Basil Petrov,
who makes everything seem possible.

Acknowledgments

First and foremost, I would like to acknowledge my parents, Sue and Radha Prasad, for their unwavering love and support. Thanks, also, to Bill Adler, who gave me the opportunity to write this book, and to Lilly Golden, who read and reread these pages with keenness, dedication, and good humor. Finally, I would like to thank my agent, Rosalie Siegel, for always being both gracious and tenacious.

Table of Contents

Introduction

WHY THE JOB MARKET NEEDS OUTWITTING

Let's face it: When confronted with the prospect of job-hunting, many of us react with bleary-eyed misery, a desire for prolonged napping, and frequent trips to the local video store. No one relishes constructing a résumé, or editing a cover letter for the umpteenth time, or calling close friends and distant relatives alike for leads. At the same time, confronting the job market is inevitable. Like death and taxes, looking for work is a necessary evil in a world where comfort and well-being are defined by a steady salary.

But if a great job is so important, why are we skittish about exploring our employment options? Maybe because the job market is often frightening.

One-time stalwarts like Xerox, WorldCom, Kmart, and Polaroid, struggling to stay afloat, have shed their workers like extra baggage. Hundreds of start-ups have tanked, leaving thousands of workers to rely on unemployment benefits and their bare wits. Governments are chopping their payrolls, and not even the Chairman of the Federal Reserve Board can predict with any certainty when a bear market will turn bullish, or vice versa. Even in better times, many employees are overworked and underpaid, facing inept managers, sub-par working conditions, or the possibility of unexpected downsizing.

The message is clear. Even the safest companies can succumb to stock market fluctuations, economic slow-downs, funding limitations, strong industry rivals, or poor management. Even the safest jobs aren't so safe.

But there is an upside. Outwitting the job market may never be as pleasant as drinking a cool glass of lemonade on a hot summer day. But it doesn't have to be scary, either. The trick is to investigate your industry, plot your strategy, meticulously prepare your applications materials, and plan for the occasional setback. If you do these things—and do them correctly—you will not only outwit the job market in the immediate future, but also learn tricks for long-term triumph. After all, a true job market virtuoso knows that the process never stops. Even if you've already found a wonderful position, it never hurts to keep your fingers in the pot in case of better offers.

What, then, do you need to take the job market by storm? This book will tell you all the essentials, from your earliest research efforts to negotiating your salary once an offer rolls in. You'll learn the basics on résumé and cover letter construction, the lowdown on networking, tricks on how to master the most difficult interview questions, and tactics for enhancing your marketability. You'll read canny advice from human resources personnel, career counselors, managers, recruiters, and interviewers from companies large and small, public and private. You'll hear tips from jobseekers who have already tracked down and captured fantastic positions. You'll also learn from other people's mistakes—what *not* to do along the path to your dream job.

This book is for everyone—from new graduates scouting for their first jobs, to career changers, to established professionals who have been laid off or are just looking to assess their options. You'll find exercises, anecdotes, examples, and strategies that can be put to use immediately. Every chapter contains hands-on ideas designed to help you tackle real job market obstacles. Armed with these tried-and-true techniques, you will be able to outsmart your competition, impress employers, and in time, land a job that truly fits your personal and professional needs.

Chapter One

FIRST THINGS FIRST:
TAKING INVENTORY

Getting started—it's often the hardest part of any new project. But treating the job search like a project or even a hobby is usually the best way to proceed. If you're currently in school, think of the job search as an additional class, complete with homework assignments and class time. If you're in the workforce but scouting for another position, or if you've lost your job and are on the lookout for a new one, the job search will require the same type of consistent effort. Allotting a period of time each day to the process is imperative because if left to our own devices, many of us would be more likely to make a dentist appointment than to sit at a computer and sift through online job postings. By regularly devoting a slot of time each day—a half hour is good, a full hour is even better—you'll stand a better chance of success in your search than by, say, skimming the classifieds of your local paper every other Sunday. So mark your calendar or daily planner—and be sure to stick to whatever schedule you make.

But really, is this kind of dedication necessary?

In a word, yes! A senior graphic designer at a major automotive club calls the job search "a game of numbers," and she's absolutely right. Many jobseekers don't realize that major companies are likely to receive hundreds, even thousands, of applications for a single position, especially if that position is posted on a popular online career portal like Monster (www.monster.com) or HotJobs (www.hotjobs.com). A human resources (HR) manager at a leading IT (information technology) provider admits, "We have a Website where people can submit résumés into an electronic database. [But this database offers] a very slim chance of getting in the door." He goes on to say that he can count on one hand the number of times he has turned to the database, which means that some perfectly qualified candidates didn't get noticed. The situation isn't fair, but it's the way many businesses operate. HR personnel simply don't have the time to wade through a waist-high pile of résumés.

Obviously, getting noticed is a major step in outwitting the job market. And the only way to get noticed is to invest a good bit of time and effort in the process. But where do you begin?

The best way to start is with a self-assessment outlining precisely what you have to offer an employer and what you're looking for in one. Without clarification, your job search can become dizzyingly broad, leading you along paths you wouldn't otherwise take. Ben O'Connell, a producer in the programming operations division of a public affairs network, says that applying for positions was difficult until he fine-tuned his search. "I looked through a lot of Internet resources and . . . went to the San Francisco public library to look through the numerous materials they had. In the end I didn't find any of them useful. I was much more successful when I targeted a specific company and pursued a specific job rather than taking a shotgun approach."

O'Connell's experience isn't unusual. If you can effectively narrow the range of your search and begin the process with a clear mission, you will be infinitely more likely to succeed. Even if you're an established professional and already have a distinct career path in mind, it never hurts to reassess yourself in the face of an ever-changing job market. In fact, some of the most successful professionals routinely undergo self-appraisals to make sure they're on target professionally and that their short- and long-term goals are realistic.

To begin your own Personal Career Inventory, take pen to paper (or use a program like Microsoft Excel) and follow the steps below.

Creating a Personal Career Inventory

STEP ONE: THINK ABOUT WHAT YOU HAVE TO OFFER

Here, you will need to write down what you have to offer an employer, including industry expertise, skills and training, and your educational background. If this is your first job search or if you don't have prior work experience, focus on more innate skills. For example, you might be a top-notch oral and written communicator, or perhaps you demonstrated strong leadership skills while pursuing volunteer work.

Don't forget to include skills that might not be immediately apparent. In fact, some of the skills that are most important to employers might not seem crucial to a jobseeker. Says Justin Moore, a professional looking for employment with a financial institution, "One manager asked me if I ever interacted with the IT department of my last employer. I had many times, especially when I was establishing the requirements and specifications for a certain project. But I'd never thought to add that information to my résumé."

As businesses become more global, knowledge of a foreign language—or even knowledge of the culture and business practices of a certain country—can be a real asset. Kathleen Pierce, a former ESL (English as a Second Language) teacher, says that a working knowledge of Russian was one of the reasons she was hired as a teacher. A large percentage of her students were from the former Soviet Union.

Are you Internet savvy? Can you find your way around basic HTML (hypertext markup language)? If so, say so. Have you done freelance work in your field or in a related field? Some of your most compelling work experience might not necessarily have come from your last regular job. Are you a member of any professional or trade associations? Employers may look favorably upon such affiliations, especially if you've attended related seminars or lectures. Membership to such organizations may show both a flair for networking and a commitment to continuing education and professional advancement.

Don't forget to consider internship experience too, even if you're not looking for an entry-level position. Shawn Jarrett, an MBA who now works as a manager of strategic alliances for Pitney Bowes, went directly from his undergraduate institution to business school. He stresses how important a summer internship was to the early stages of his professional career. "For those coming out of school with no experience," he says, "beg, steal, or borrow, but make sure you get an internship within your field." Indeed, most employers like to see solid work experience on your résumé, even if it takes the form of an internship.

STEP TWO: CONSIDER WHAT WOULD MAKE YOU HAPPY IN A JOB

For this step, there are two categories to consider. First, the bottom line: What industry do you want to work in, what kind of companies do you wish to target, and how much money do you want to make? And second, beyond the basics, which work-related factors are important to you and to your personal lifestyle? Such factors might include a brief commute, stable hours, overtime pay, a hands-off manager, a great health care plan, your own office, company stability, a great 401(k) plan, on-site childcare, an on-site gym, relocation assistance, employee diversity, or company-sponsored education and training.

Bill Waldorf, an MBA and licensed counselor with a certification in career counseling, says that "values, both personal and career-related, may be the most crucial factor in evaluating if people are fulfilled in their work, especially as they get older." More important than even a great paycheck? Absolutely, says one Connecticut-based computer analyst, who took a sizable pay cut in order to work in the public sector. "In looking for my job, I was more concerned with location," he says. "I was looking for a lifestyle change. [Ideally,] I wanted to work at a large university that was within biking distance."

Focus, too, on what you wouldn't want in a job. Anyone who has been in the workplace long enough has dealt with a boss who might as well be the second coming of Godzilla: temperamental, overbearing, and prone to fiery outbursts. Yet a good boss, one who is also a mentor and has your long-term career prospects in mind, can make all the difference. Other factors that might turn off a person to a specific job: a very casual atmosphere or a very formal one, a lack of corporate vision, too many layers of bureaucracy—the list goes on and on. What might send *you* running from a position?

A final thought: In tough economic times, it's not uncommon for a person to jump at his or her first job offer. Sometimes, it has to be this way. The bills are piling up, you're subsisting on mac and cheese, and those unemployment checks are almost up. If you're sleeping on your Great-Aunt Ethel's couch, survival is probably more important than job satisfaction. But if you do have a little wiggle room, consider what would make you content in the workplace. It's common sense, after all. Happy people are more likely to perform well at their jobs.

STEP THREE: FUNNEL IT DOWN TO THE ESSENTIALS

Ideally, in your search for a job, you will find a position that fits all the criteria you listed above. However, in the tumultuous world of employment you'll probably have to make some concessions. Some of these concessions you would be able to cope with; others you wouldn't. The key is knowing the difference. Perhaps there are certain skills that you are passionate about using on the job. Perhaps you know that nothing would make you happier than to work at a specific company, even if you have to start in a less-than-ideal position. Perhaps you have a family, and a short commute and child-friendly benefits are of utmost importance to you. Only you know for sure how to distinguish a priority from a perk.

One employee said that the only thing he required of his next employer was an efficient management team. He explains, "Previously, I had worked for Internet companies with a philosophy of 'ready, fire, aim' instead of 'ready, aim, fire.' Their projects would just spin out of control. . . . I wanted [to work for a company] that did a lot of planning." Another jobseeker who just finished a back-to-back bachelor's degree and graduate degree in journalism knew that she needed a position within a certain salary range in order to pay her monthly rent, bills, *and* hefty student loans.

With your own personal needs in mind, write down what a job must have in order for you to accept it.

STEP FOUR: KNOW WHERE YOU STAND

You can't know exactly where you fall in the job applicant schema, but you can determine your general standing. Are you fresh out of school, or are you experienced—looking for a job in a field that you have worked in before? Are you hoping to cross over to a different career sector? Perhaps you are looking for work in a new field but have highly transferable skills.

Knowing where you stand means knowing what types of positions you are eligible for. It is advantageous for you to determine what jobs would be most appropriate given your education, skills, and prior work experience *before* you start the application process. Why? Because not knowing this information and applying to every position under the sun will only waste your time and the time of harried hiring managers. A good rule of thumb for determining this information is to consider the title you held at your last position and to look at or above that level. Haven't had a job before? Looking to start work in a new field? Here's where informational interviews can provide you with some direction (see "Going on Informational Interviews," page 12). If you're in college, take advantage of your school's career resources center. A conversation with a professional there can help you to evaluate where you might best fit within your desired field.

Knowing where you stand will also help you to tweak your résumé and cover letter accordingly. Leigh Wetzel, the online manager of a paper goods company, explains, "I've found that putting [certain] skills on my résumé, specifically computer programs that I know, can work against me. Those skills put me in the category of 'worker' rather than 'manager.' Managers manage people and projects, and I wouldn't want the hiring manager [at a prospective employer] to mistake my résumé [as targeted for] for a lesser position." Knowing what level of responsibility she is capable of assuming, and knowing that companies would consider her for this level only if she presented herself in a certain way, Wetzel gave herself an edge on the competition. Many people make the mistake of sending out résumés and cover letters without thinking from a potential employer's perspective.

So give it a try. Write down a list of job titles and/or department areas that are appropriate for your experience, education, and skill set. And keep in mind that the process of determining where you stand isn't an exact science, especially in a rough job market when many people take jobs they wouldn't opt for in a better economy.

After completing this inventory, keep it close to your desk or wherever you plan to carry out your job search efforts. In Chapter 2, it will become a useful tool in shaping and refining the scope of your search.

Example: Personal Career Inventory

Alicia Jimenez: Journalist (college graduate looking for first job)

WHAT I HAVE TO OFFER AN EMPLOYER

✓ College graduate from the University of Florida in Gainesville with a BA in Journalism. Graduation date: May 2003. GPA: 3.4

✓ Summer internship with the *Daily Tribune* in 2002

✓ Received merit scholarship from the Florida Press League in 2001

✓ Fluent in Spanish

✓ Features Writer/Editor for my college newspaper from September 2002 to May 2003

✓ Reporter for my college newspaper from September 2001 to May 2002.

✓ I know Microsoft Office, basic HTML, Adobe Photoshop, and Adobe PageMaker. I am very good at performing research using the Internet

✓ Courses taken include Advanced Newspaper Design, Advanced Magazine Composition and Layout, and Intermediate Copywriting

✓ Current member of the Society of Environmental Journalists

✓ Volunteer at the Student Crisis Hotline Center from 2001 to 2003

✓ Waitress at Margie's Café while I was in high school

WHAT WOULD MAKE ME HAPPY IN A JOB

✓ A job with a reputable and established newspaper

✓ A job that includes lots of field work and on-site reporting

✓ A boss who is also a mentor—someone who will give me every opportunity to challenge myself and to learn and grow professionally

✓ Regular writing and editing assignments

✓ A salary at or above $25,000

✓ A great health care plan

✓ A culturally diverse working environment

✓ A job located in Florida

THE ESSENTIALS

✓ An entry-level or above editorial position with a reputable newspaper

✓ A professional environment that is a good fit with my personality and working style

- ✓ A job where I can use any of my core skills, including writing, editing, and/or research
- ✓ A job located in Florida

WHERE I STAND

- ✓ Because this is my first job out of college, I am most likely to get an entry-level position with a title of Reporter or Staff Reporter
- ✓ I will probably have to do some administrative duties until I have proven myself and am deemed worthy of assuming greater responsibility

Example: Personal Career Inventory

Jonathan Hope: Marketing Professional - MBA graduate

WHAT I HAVE TO OFFER AN EMPLOYER

- ✓ Over five years of experience in direct marketing, strategic planning, promotions, and marketing communications
- ✓ Proven ability in conducting market and customer research to identify new trends
- ✓ Ability to manage and to delegate responsibilities, as demonstrated in my current position as Associate Marketing Director of the FLR Corporation in Atlanta, Georgia
- ✓ Received the United States Marketing Association's Excellence Award for Creative Vision in 2002
- ✓ Received the Georgia Marketing Association's Crystal Award in 2001
- ✓ MBA from the Terry College of Business in Athens, Georgia. GPA: 3.6

✓ BS in Economics from the University of Tennessee in Knoxville, Tennessee. Minor in Political Science. GPA: 3.8
✓ Highly motivated, diligent, a self-starter, and a team player
✓ Exceptional oral and written communication skills

WHAT WOULD MAKE ME HAPPY IN A JOB

✓ A small- to medium-size company that is in a stage of high growth
✓ A position that will grant me direct communication with the executive ranks
✓ A position that will enable me to lead the marketing team
✓ A position that will enable me to oversee the marketing process from early marketing research through to marketing communication
✓ A solid benefits package
✓ Restricted travel—no more than one extended business trip per month
✓ A commute of no longer than thirty minutes
✓ A salary increase of at least 10 percent

THE ESSENTIALS

✓ A position that is a step up from my current job in terms of title and overall responsibility
✓ A position that will enable me to manage all aspects of marketing in the company
✓ A small- to medium-size company that is stable and growing
✓ A salary increase of at least 10 percent

WHERE I STAND

✓ Given that I am currently the Associate Marketing Director of a medium-size company, I am hoping to climb to the position of Director of Marketing at a company of similar–or slightly smaller–size

✓ For the sake of security, I won't quit my current job until I have locked in a position with another company. If my job search is not successful after six months, I will stay with my current employer, but will try to take on more diverse projects so that I can strengthen my management abilities

Help—I Don't Know My Future Career Plans!

There are some people who have known since childhood what they want to be and who have worked their whole lives toward becoming zoologists, criminal prosecutors, classical musicians, or gourmet chefs. On the flip side there are people who have never had that "eureka!" moment. When it comes to career goals, they're stuck in a state of perpetual indecision—or waffling.

Some people are notorious wafflers—they've never been sure of which career direction to take and they're skittish about making any firm decisions, lest those decisions turn out to be the wrong ones. Other people waffle only occasionally. Maybe they've been in one profession for a number of years and have decided that they want to try something else, but don't quite know what that something else is. Or maybe they've finished school and are reluctant to commit themselves to a field that they're not sure about. There are even those souls who have a flair for too many things—their talents are evenly spread in various areas—and they don't know where to concentrate.

At best, waffling is an uncomfortable state of being. At worst, it can turn into full-fledged anxiety, unloading massive amounts of stress onto its victim. Fortunately, if you're willing to do a bit of legwork, there are many good ways of identifying and researching a job or career direction. You probably won't come to a decision right away regarding the rest of your life. But by trying these suggestions, you will at least be able to eliminate those areas that aren't a good fit for you. And that's not a bad place to start.

GOING ON INFORMATIONAL INTERVIEWS

An informational interview is exactly what it sounds like—an interview arranged for the purpose of gathering information. Informational interviews are ideal for the person who is thinking of starting a career in a new sector, but who wants to hear from an insider what that sector is really like. Say you are interested in learning more about careers in accounting. The best way to start is by contacting an accountant, explaining that you are interested in learning more about her job, and politely asking for a half-hour of her time.

Don't know an accountant? No problem. Think of the "Six Degrees of Separation" theory, which supposes that each person is separated from the next by no more than five others. That's something of an exaggeration in the workforce, where lines of communication and information are continually intersecting; there may be no more than one or two people separating you from a prospective informational interviewer. Ask family members, friends, neighbors, and other contacts if they know someone who works in the area that interests you, and chances are good that you'll receive a name and phone number.

But even if you come up short, "cold calling"—or picking up the yellow pages and dialing a few numbers—isn't a bad option. You may be surprised by how much some people enjoy speaking about their jobs. David Wittenberg, a manager of technology planning, explains, "When you demonstrate sincere concern for someone's interests, it motivates the other person to want to help you." If your informational interviewer seems especially avid and agreeable, you might even ask to "shadow" him for an hour or even a day to see firsthand what his working life is like.

For more information on networking and informational interviews, see chapter 3.

TEMPING

Becoming a temporary employee—or "temping," as it is more commonly called—is not a notion that warms the cockles of most people's hearts. In fact, it can conjure nightmarish images of endless clerical work and coffee-making. But the upside to temping is that you're not committing yourself to one company or even to one industry. Temps are outsiders, and the glorious part about being an outsider is that you are free to observe and assess your surroundings without being committed to them. In other words, temping offers a steep learning curve by giving you direct access to many employers for limited periods of time—no strings attached.

If you're unemployed and undecided about what your next job should be, temping can help you to make decisions about which types of companies best fit your personality and working style. Who knows? You may strike gold and end up temping at a company that you really love. If you work hard enough and capture the respect of the employees around you, you may even land a full-time offer. It happens. One Manhattan-based jobseeker, who sent out over 100 résumés before deciding to approach several temporary staffing agencies, explains, "I was reluctant at first. I had always thought of temping as a worst-case scenario. But that's the way I got my foot in the door of [trade journal] publishing."

VISITING A CAREER COUNSELOR

Okay—so what exactly are career counselors? Think of them as career psychics, only instead of using crystal balls and tarot cards, they use rigorous tests in order to match an individual's interests and personality to logical and suitable career options. Different career counselors, also called "career advisors" or "career coaches," offer different services, but most are ultimately working to empower their clients to make informed decisions regarding their careers.

How do they do it? A career counselor will likely use a gamut of written and verbal assessment tools. Some of the most common tools are the Strong Interest Inventory and the Myers-Briggs Type Indicator, but there are many others. These assessments are used to collect and quantify information on a person's skills and abilities, educational development, interpersonal style, and values. Using this information, your counselor will then work with you on how to clarify and pursue your career goals. Your counselor may also offer one-on-one or group consultation sessions, administer relevant assignments, provide analysis of marketability, and work with you on a myriad of other employment-related exercises.

Career counselors, says Bill Waldorf, are useful for a number of people, including but not limited to those who are just out of high school or college but unsure about their place in the workforce, long-time professionals who have grown disenchanted with their job situations, and workers looking to reenter the workforce after being attendant parents.

Before you jump into a relationship with a career counselor, it pays to do a bit of investigative work. Waldorf, who has a private practice in a northern Atlanta suburb, says the best counselor is usually "somebody who has career credentials, counseling credentials, and who takes a diverse and integrative approach in terms of the assessment. Assessments are tools, but not everything. You also want a career counselor who tailors their approach to you as a person, given your needs and your personality." It's a good idea to get certain facts up front, such as information on services and fees, ethical guidelines, and time commitments. Some counselors offer one-time sessions. Others will want to see their clients on a regular basis for several weeks or more.

A good place to learn more about career counselors is at the Website of the National Career Development Association (NCDA), a division of the American Counseling Association (ACA). Visit www.ncda.org.

DOING RELEVANT READING

Open up just about any fashion magazine and you'll probably see some do-it-yourself test on what you should do with your career (alongside articles on how you can find your soul mate and the best way to condition your hair). Such articles are not relevant to the person who is serious about outwitting the job market. Fortunately, there is a spate of insightful books out there for people who are keen on exploring their personal career possibilities. Perhaps the best known and most respected is *What Color Is Your Parachute?* by Richard Nelson Bolles. First appearing in 1970, *Parachute* has since been translated into ten languages and updated many times to keep up with the shifting needs of jobseekers. It includes a meticulous step-by-step plan for identifying a new career and pursuing it. It is theoretical in approach, but practical in the sense that is asks readers to do quite a bit of self-exploration before making critical career-related decisions. More proof of *Parachute's* influence: The Library of Congress named it one of the "25 Books That Have Shaped Readers' Lives."

Another crucial place for career-relevant reading is the newest *Occupational Outlook Handbook* by the United States Department of Labor. Revised and updated each year, the handbook offers a summary of hundreds of positions, from lodging manager, to accountant, to taxi driver, to funeral director, to anything and everything in between. In each summary you will find information on the nature of the position, working conditions, required training and qualifications, earnings, and perhaps most importantly, the job outlook. Find out if your prospective sector is expected to experience job growth or decline—vital information for anyone concerned with career longevity. Be sure, too, to visit the "Tomorrow's Jobs" section of the *Handbook,* which gives a general overview of the industries that are on the make—and on the break. In the 2002-3 edition of the *Handbook*, for example, the transportation, communications, and utilities sector is expected to increase by 1.3 million jobs by 2010, while farmers and ranchers are expected to experience sizable employment decline.

NOTE: For a fee, you can buy a paperback or hardcover edition of the *Occupational Outlook Handbook*. Visit the Department of Labor Website for ordering information (www.dol.gov).

TAKING A CLASS

Taking a class in a sector that interests you is a useful way to get your feet wet before plunging in. Taking classes is particularly useful if your prospective field requires an undergraduate or graduate degree. Consider taking one or more classes in the sector before plunking down thousands of dollars in full tuition. Some schools will even allow you to audit a class for free—meaning that you can sit in on the lectures or seminars, but not actively participate. Call the admissions departments of the schools in your area for more information.

While regular classes offer people a familiar academic setting, online classes, such as those offered at the University of Phoenix's Online University (www.uoponline.com), are great for people who need flexibility in terms of studying and class time. Online classes work much like regular classes do, except that all your activities— registering, submitting assignments, interacting with classmates, communicating with your professors, etc.—are done via computer. The advantage is that you never have to leave the cozy confines of your home, although some students say that unwavering motivation is necessary to weather the absence of face-to-face interaction.

Don't forget that in times of economic slow-down, when jobs are scarce, more people opt to return to graduate school, making admission more competitive.

Key Chapter Points

✦ Outwitting the job market will require a consistent and concerted effort. Set aside a block of time each day for the process.

✦ Creating a Personal Career Inventory will help you to narrow the scope of your job search. The following four steps are essential: think about what you have to offer, consider what would make you happy in a position, funnel it down to the essentials, and know where you stand with potential employers.

✦ If you're unsure of your future career plans, the following methods can help you to pare down your options: going on informational interviews, trying a temporary staffing position, visiting a career counselor, doing career-related reading, and taking a class in your prospective sector.

Chapter Two

WHERE DO I START?
BEGINNING YOUR SEARCH

If you've finished your Personal Career Inventory and set aside a block of time each day for your employment search, you're on your way. The next step is using your inventory to determine which companies you should target.

Many of us will research a company only after we've been asked to come in for an interview; starting any earlier seems like a waste. But surprisingly, researching companies before you apply for jobs will save you time and energy in the long run. You will gain more insight into which potential employers are a good fit and which you're better off avoiding. By early researching, you'll also avoid a common jobseeker pitfall: coming into an interview without fully understanding the internal workings of the company.

After she finished college Kathleen Pierce, a former ESL instructor, had several interviews in New York City for paralegal positions. Yet because she had so many interviews in such a short period, she didn't have enough time to research each individual law firm. One interviewer sensed this and said, "If you didn't take the time to learn about this company, then don't waste my time. This interview is over. Have a nice day." Pierce learned a valuable lesson from her experience. She explains, "There are many law firms around the city, but there is always something that makes a place unique—[it's critical to] find out what that is." Indeed, performing in-depth company research offers two advantages: you'll be better prepared to give informed responses during interviews, and you'll be equipped to compare and contrast potential employers.

Here's where your Personal Career Inventory comes in. You have already consolidated the vital information—what you have to offer an employer and what kind of company you're looking for. Now it's a matter of matching this information to select companies.

Creating a Prospective Employer List

Some people already know the company that would best suit them. One human resources professional knew from the age of sixteen that she wanted to work for General Electric. She had long been enamored of the company's mission and history, and also of the charisma of former chairman and CEO, John F. Welch. Yet most people are a bit more equivocal. They know their preferred industry or sector, but not much else.

If you know only your industry, it's a good idea to use the information on your Personal Career Inventory to pick ten or more potential companies in your field. Maybe they are large corporations that have name brand recognition or that offer more job security than smaller companies or new enterprises would. Maybe they are within an easy commuting distance. Maybe you know already that they are hiring in your field. Or maybe they are companies that you've heard positive things about through friends or relatives.

Keep in mind that the employers you pick don't have to have every criterion listed on your Personal Career Inventory. But all of them should have a few things in their favor, and all of them should be companies that you think are worthy of further investigation. Once you have determined these prospective companies, create a Prospective Employer List. Jot down notes about the "pros" and "cons" of each company as you perform your research. Also leave a space entitled "Notes." Here, you can track your job application progress, which is discussed on page 107.

Example: Prospective Employer List

Alicia Jimenez: Journalist (college graduate looking for first job)

POTENTIAL EMPLOYER

The *Daily Tribune* (Location: Gainesville, Florida)

PROS

✓ I had a summer internship there and am familiar with the work environment

✓ My supervisor, who thought I did a good job during my internship, might be willing to give me a referral

✓ I would have a short commute

✓ I wouldn't need to relocate

✓ The paper's readership base is expanding, which is probably a sign of the company's financial stability

CONS

✓ A new Editor-in-Chief onboard means that the paper might experience a rocky transitional period

✓ The employment page of the company website lists only jobs in Sales and Marketing at this time

✓ My friend Louise, a former copywriter at the paper, says that the benefits are below average compared with the benefits of similar employers

✓ During my internship I worked unusually long hours and some weekends. A full-time job with the company would probably mean equally long hours

NOTES: _____

_____

_____

POTENTIAL EMPLOYER

The *Florida Daily News* (Location: Tampa, Florida)

PROS

✓ One of Florida's most widely read and most respected papers

✓ Among journalists, the *Florida Daily News* is generally regarded as the best paper to work for in the state

✓ The work environment is intense and I would probably have a steep learning curve

✓ ReporterToday.com named this paper one of the top fifty to work for in the country

✓ Because I have a subscription to this paper, I'm familiar with the style of the reporting and the types of articles that are published

CONS

✓ I would need to relocate

✓ Because of its popularity, many people apply to jobs at this paper. I would face lots of competition trying to get a job there

✓ The salaries are lower at this paper than at others, especially for entry-level positions

✓ Because I don't have any friends or family in Tampa, I won't have much of a social network or support system there

✓ A contact at the *Florida Daily News* has told me that the paper seldom hires recent college graduates with GPAs below 3.6

✓ Because the paper is so large and established, I might not have the editorial opportunities I would probably have at a smaller paper

NOTES: _____

_____

_____

_____

Example: Prospective Employer List

Jonathan Hope: MBA (Associate Director of Marketing looking for Director of Marketing position)

POTENTIAL EMPLOYER

Magic Fountain Multimedia (Location: Brooklyn, NY)

PROS

✓ Magic Fountain Multimedia has a positive cash flow. The company has steadily increased its earnings and dividends paid in the last three years

✓ According to the CEO's address to shareholders in the last annual report, the company is beginning to offer its services to companies outside the United States, thus increasing its clientele and overall visibility

✓ Most of the clients of Magic Fountain Multimedia are Fortune 500 companies

✓ Good benefits and pension plan

✓ In this tumultuous job market, Magic Fountain is more stable than my present employer

CONS

✓ Even though the position is a step up in hierarchy, it would not offer as many responsibilities as my present position does

✓ I would need to relocate

✓ Brooklyn is a slightly more expensive place to live than Atlanta, Georgia

✓ Because Magic Fountain Multimedia is a medium-size company, there may be more bureaucracy than at a smaller company

NOTES: _____

_____

_____

_____

POTENTIAL EMPLOYER

The Altbridge Group (Location: Atlanta, Georgia)

PROS

✓ Because The Altbridge Group is a small company, I would have more responsibility and decision-making power

✓ I'm already somewhat familiar with way Altbridge conducts business because I collaborated with the company on a former project

✓ Because the company appears to be in decline, if I were to get the job and help to turn the company around, my sense of accomplishment would be greater than if I were to work at a company that is already doing well

✓ The Altbridge Group has an employee bonus plan tied to performance with evaluations done on a semi-annual basis

✓ I would have a short commute

✓ I wouldn't need to relocate

CONS

✓ Because The Altbridge Group is a private company, there is no public information available on its strategic, financial, and operational outlook

✓ According to one online careers site, The Altbridge Group has been losing clients to larger and more prominent competitors

✓ Because it is a private company, there is a chance that the owners might override decisions made by hired professionals or otherwise interfere with day-to-day operations

✓ The salary for Director of Marketing at The Altbridge Group may not be as high as the salaries for similar positions at larger companies

NOTES: _____

_____

_____

_____

Where to Conduct Your Research

For the sake of example, let's say you are interested in a specific position in the pharmaceutical industry. The first company on your Prospective Employer List is Johnson & Johnson. Perhaps you already know a little about Johnson & Johnson—it's a well-known manufacturer of health care products, after all. But how can you get your hands on all the vital details? Use the techniques below to gather the necessary information, especially that of hiring practices and job availability in your field.

THE OFFICIAL COMPANY WEBSITE

Official company literature, both printed and online, usually provides a basic platform of knowledge. On the Johnson & Johnson Website (www.jnj.com), for example, you can learn about the company's history, its family of products, its umbrella of national and international businesses, its latest news and press releases, and then some. All of this information is interesting—and much of it may be relevant—but as a jobseeker, the first thing you want to know is if the company is hiring professionals in your field. On Johnson & Johnson's Website that information is listed under the heading of "Careers." On other company Websites it may be listed under "Jobs," or "Join Our Team," or "Work at Our Company," or any number of other variations—so search carefully. When you do find the career page, be sure to pay special attention to the general information on hiring and recruiting. Many companies, such as those in the consulting or investment banking industries, do the bulk of their hiring from the applicant pools of specific colleges, universities, and business schools. You'll want to know if your educational background fits the bill.

If you don't see any openings that match your credentials, don't disregard the company just yet. Many employers don't post all their open positions—they first try to fill them through internal candidates and employee referrals. So if you're still interested in the company after perusing its Website, keep it on your Prospective Employer List.

Keep in mind, too, that a company's Website is a way of advertising—so you are unlikely to see any negative information on the company here. For a more objective overview, you'll have to use other resources too.

FINANCIAL REPORTS (FOR PUBLICLY TRADED COMPANIES)

A jobseeker can learn a great deal about a company by glancing at its financial reports. A company like Johnson & Johnson, which is publicly traded, is required by the Securities and Exchange Commission (SEC) to report its financial results for each year. These results generally contain balance sheets, income and cash flow statements, descriptions of company operations, and—importantly for jobseekers—commentaries on the outlook for the future. Much of the time a public company's quarterly, midyear, or annual reports will be posted right on its Website. If not, the annual reports for public companies and mutual funds in the United States are available for free on the SEC's Website at www.sec.gov.

Daunting as the reports may seem at first glance, you don't have to be a financial expert to decode them. A five- or ten-minute skim will help you to determine if the company is financially sound. If the company is posting profits and has displayed steady growth over the last several years, then chances are it is holding strong. On the other hand, an unusual event or uncertain outlook may signal trouble. Maybe the company has not met quarterly expectations, or its CEO is stepping down, or it is unable to make its scheduled interest payments, or its board is about to vote on a merger. In times of financial turbulence, a company may be more interested in slashing jobs than in filling them, so make a note on your Prospective Employer List of any unusual activity you find.

NOTE: Private companies, or companies whose shares are not traded on the open market, are not obliged to publicly disclose their financial data. Therefore, if you are trying to unearth information on such a company, you will have to be a little bit more creative in your approach.

BUSINESS AND CAREER PERIODICALS

If the thought of financial reports gives you the willies, you can always rely on reputable print and online media. Respected publications like *The New York Times* (www.nytimes.com), the *Wall Street Journal* (www.wsj. com), *Financial Times* (www.ft.com), *Forbes* (www.forbes.com), *Fortune* (www.fortune.com), *The Economist* (www.economist.com), and *BusinessWeek* (www. businessweek.com) all cover major company news—mergers and acquisitions, new product launches, earnings reports, management shifts, etc. In some cases, you can circumvent the subscription fee by visiting these publications online, where a quick registration is all you need to access the articles. Your city or town library may also carry many—if not all—of the above newspapers and periodicals.

CAREER WEBSITES

Career Websites are yet another useful tool for company sleuthing. Many of the sites purport to obtain their information from actual employees, so you may learn the skinny on more targeted issues, anything from dress codes, to what questions are often asked by interviewers, to the quality of the food in a company's cafeteria.

Although there are many career sites out there, some of the more distinguished include Vault (www.vault.com), Hoover's (www.hoovers. com), and Wetfeet (www.wetfeet.com). Simply type in

"Johnson & Johnson" on Vault, for example, and you will find out that the company offers "more on-site childcare centers than any other company" and other important but lesser-known information.

A word of caution as you explore various online career sites: Don't rely on a single site for all your company information. Online content may be outdated, so it's best to verify the material against other sources such as business and career periodicals.

CURRENT OR FORMER EMPLOYEES

Perhaps the best way to learn both the basics and the inside secrets of a company is to chat with someone who is working there or has worked there in the recent past. Be sure to ask the questions that haven't been answered already by your other sources. A company insider may be able to reveal information that hasn't been spread to the general media, such as which departments are growing, whether the company's products or services are changing, or the best way to apply for positions.

If you don't know any company insiders, you may be able to make contacts using the networking techniques discussed in chapter 3.

Starting the Job Search

Once you've used the above techniques to sufficiently research the companies on your Prospective Employer List, you can finally start your job search. Of course, before you apply to any jobs, you'll have to perfect your résumé and cover letter. (We'll discuss how to do this in chapters 4 and 5, respectively.) But for the moment, it doesn't hurt to see what's out there.

Start by taking a good look at your Prospective Employer List. Ask yourself if all the companies still seem like strong contenders. Which are financially secure and growing? Which are hiring candidates with your credentials? Which seem most compatible with your working style and skill set? Do you know any employees at one or more of your prospective companies who may be able to help you get your foot in the door? Keep in mind that your Prospective Employer List is not static. As you search for jobs, you may find other companies that you hadn't originally considered. Conversely, you may find that one or more of the employers that you had previously considered no longer seem appealing.

While doing your research you probably noticed available jobs on the Websites of your prospective companies. Applying for positions directly through a company's site is convenient and may yield positive results. But don't limit yourself—a variety of other options awaits you.

GENERAL JOB SEARCH SITES

A huge number of jobseekers conduct their searches through third-party employment sites. The bigwigs in this area are Monster.com and HotJobs.com, each of which advertises tens of thousands of jobs in every field imaginable. The upside to using Monster or HotJobs is that they're free to use and you won't be lacking for variety—small companies and major corporations alike use Monster and HotJobs to post open positions. The drawback, however, is that because so many people are applying for the same positions, it's not easy to stand out in the crowd. Manager David Wittenberg keenly observes, "It's not unusual if you're going to send out a résumé online to be one of two thousand applicants." Still, a few intrepid jobseekers do make their way through a sea of résumés and live to tell about it. One professional who works in Providence, Rhode Island, not only cinched her present job through HotJobs, she was also invited for interviews at half a dozen other companies.

While Monster and HotJobs remain the top brass, there are several up-and-coming contenders in this field such as FlipDog (www.flipdog.com) and CareerBuilder (www.careerbuilder.com), both of which are worth a look. For new college grads, Monster offers JobTRAK (www.jobtrak.com), which partners with many colleges and universities in order to offer positions available to students of those schools. A number of senior managers suggest 6FigureJobs (www.sixfigurejobs.com), which, true to its name, advertises only high-level positions for executives looking to earn a minimum annual income of $100,000. Finally, the regionally specific and rapidly growing Craigslist (www.craigslist.org) advertises jobs in select cities, among them Phoenix, San Francisco, Miami, Houston, Boston, and Atlanta.

This is just a sampling of the many job search sites available—so don't hesitate to try your luck with the others you might hear about.

INDUSTRY-SPECIFIC JOB SEARCH SITES

A general job search site is one thing, but an industry-specific site is its own animal. Rather than catering to all jobseekers at all levels in all industries, industry-specific sites offer jobs in a specific specialty area. Dice (www.dice. com), for instance, provides online recruiting services for technology professionals. Melissa Walker, a professional living in New York City, touts Mediabistro (www.mediabistro. com) and the careers page at Time Inc. (careers.timeinc.com/careers) as promising search sites for editors, writers, and other professionals working on the creative end of publishing. On www.legaljobs.com there are law positions aplenty, and as well as links to legal recruiters and temporary legal staffing agencies.

The best way to locate good industry-specific job search sites in your field is to ask like-minded professionals what they have successfully used.

DIVERSITY JOB SEARCH SITES

Some job search sites cater to the professional rather than to the field. As the workforce becomes increasingly diverse, companies are eager to create staffs that reflect the many faces of the clients they are serving. This sort of commitment to diversity makes good business sense. "Futurework: Trends and Challenges for Work in the 21st Century," a report from the Department of Labor, projects that by 2050, minorities will rise from being one in every four Americans to almost one in every two. Catalyst, a nonprofit advisory organization working to advance women in business (www.catalystwomen.org), reminds us that although women comprise roughly half the total workforce in the United States, they represent only a tiny fraction of CEOs in the Fortune 500.

It's practical, then, for some professionals to look for companies that have a known track record for hiring and promoting diverse candidates. Since 1986 *Working Mother Magazine* (www.workingmother.com) has put out an annual list of the "100 Best Companies for Working Mothers." The Gay Financial Network (www.gfn.com) offers employment support services for gay and lesbian professionals. A site called IMDiversity (www.imdiversity.com) serves the career-related interests of women, as well as African Americans, Native Americans, Asian Americans, and Hispanic Americans. Other noteworthy sites for minorities include the National Society of Hispanic MBAS (www.nshmba.org), the National Black MBA Association (www.nbmbaa.org), and the United Negro College Fund (www.uncf.org).

The sites listed here are just the tip of the iceberg. There are many other reputable work-related Websites that have the best interests of diverse professionals in mind.

RECRUITERS

Recruiters, also called headhunters, are consultants who work with a client company to find qualified candidates for positions within that company. They are scouts, if you will, scouring the employment landscape for professionals who would potentially fit an organization's needs. Recruiters earn their money through the companies for whom they're recruiting—*not* through jobseekers.

There are temporary placement recruiters, permanent placement recruiters, general recruiters who work with companies in many industries, and recruiters who work exclusively in one field such as advertising, biotechnology, or pharmaceuticals. Retained recruiters have an exclusive arrangement with an employer and they receive payments for their search at the beginning of an assignment. Contingent recruiters, on the other hand, work without a retainer on an assignment and earn money only if one of their candidates is hired. Finally, corporate recruiters are employees of a given company—not outside consultants.

Although there are thousands of recruiters across the nation, they are not for everyone. Some professionals prefer to go it alone in the job search. Others may not be easy to place because of their skill set, educational background, or previous employment history.

But using a recruiter can have its advantages. A recruiter may have access to key decision-makers within an organization. She may also have knowledge of positions that are not yet advertised. Says Beth Camp, the owner of Two Roads Placement Service: "In many cases, the recruiter may have an exclusive on the position and the only way to even be considered for the job is to be submitted through the recruiter." A savvy and well-established recruiter can also market a candidate to a hiring manager before the two ever meet. In terms of salary negotiation, too, using a recruiter can be advantageous. Beth Camp continues, "The recruiter knows if there's stiff competition, whether or not the company has flexibility in salary or benefits (options, signing bonuses, guaranteeing bonuses, offering extra vacation time, guaranteeing salary reviews, etc.). If a recruiter knows how badly the client wants the candidate and what it might be willing to pay to get [him], the candidate can get a better sense of how far to push before the company pulls the offer and moves on."

Ultimately, though, the recruiter must make sure both parties have ample knowledge of the other. One recruiting consultant at a global consulting firm specializing in executive placements and board director appointments says, "My job is to see that both sides know what they're getting into. The candidate should know the expectations of their role and what it takes to be successful. The client should know who this person is, what their strengths and weaknesses are, where they'll need support, and what kind of team they'll need around them." She stresses the importance of an open and honest line of communication between all parties. She also advocates a realistic perspective when it comes to the job search: "There is no perfect candidate—there are always trade-offs, just as there is no perfect organization."

As is so often the case with employment, you can sometimes identify the best recruiters through word of mouth. Ask your friends and associates if they can recommend a good recruiter in your line of work.

EMPLOYMENT ADS

Not very long ago, the classifieds section of the local newspaper was the way most people hunted for jobs. With the advent of the Internet, that has changed. But employment ads in periodicals—including local and national newspapers, magazines, and professional and trade journals—remain one way to conduct a job search.

Bear in mind that you don't necessarily have to buy *The New York Times* or the *Wall Street Journal* to read the classifieds. These papers, and many others, are available online and offer search engines that help jobseekers pare down their searches by location, job category, job title, and/or keywords. Many online newspapers even allow jobseekers to post their résumés.

If you're not yet Internet proficient, don't fear. It's never too late to learn the tricks of online jobhunting. Below is some advice on the topic.

Getting Help with the Internet Job Search

Although the Internet is a relatively new phenomenon, the job search is now so enmeshed with the online world that jobseekers would do themselves a disservice by relying on old-fashioned methods alone.

If you're not accustomed to using the Internet, or even if you're computer-skittish, there are some fairly harmless options for learning your way around the World Wide Web. The most obvious is to ask an

Internet-savvy friend or relative for a tutorial, or better yet, for a series of tutorials. Another option is to take a course on Internet basics at your local community college. Some town and community centers also offer them—and for nominal fees. If you don't have access to an Internet-connected computer, many public libraries do. Some libraries even designate portions of their buildings specifically for career-related purposes. Yet another alternative would be to pay a computer consultant to show you the ropes. Consultants' fees and services vary, so don't forget to find out what you'll be taught in advance of your payment.

Whatever option you choose, keep in mind that the best way to find your way around the Internet is to jump right in. Spend a little time every day surfing sites of interest to you.

Key Chapter Points

- ✦ Researching companies *before* you apply for jobs will save you time and energy in the long run.

- ✦ The information on your Personal Career Inventory will help you to create an initial list of prospective employers.

- ✦ Using a combination of techniques will help you to gather necessary company information, especially that of hiring practices and job availability in your field. Try official company Websites, financial reports of publicly traded companies, business and career periodicals, career websites, and information from current or former employees.

- ✦ Utilize a variety of job search tools in addition to the official Websites of your prospective companies. Some options discussed in this chapter include general job search sites, industry-specific job search sites, diversity job search sites, recruiters, and employment ads in periodicals.

Chapter Three

NETWORK YOUR WAY INTO A JOB

Of all the chapters in *Outwitting the Job Market,* this is probably the most important one. Why? Because by unofficial count most people gain access into a company via networking. In fact, it's probably fair to say that for every person who finds a job through Monster or HotJobs, another ten find employment through people they know.

Despite its undeniable importance, networking can be intimidating. The very word can stir up disquieting images of well-groomed executives exchanging top-secret information in the confines of a boardroom or of unemployed professionals desperately calling complete strangers for help. But if the stereotypes of networking are dismal, the reality is much rosier. Dictionary.com defines networking as "an extended group of people with similar interests or concerns who interact and remain in informal contact for mutual assistance or support." This is a great definition, for it emphasizes that networking is a rather broad and amorphous concept.

Networking might very well happen in a boardroom. But it can just as easily happen in the classroom, or at a party, or even at a grocery store. Basically, any person who enters into your life may also enter into your network. A classmate you have now may later be a manager at company where you wish to work. A person you meet at a wedding or anniversary party may become instrumental in helping you to get an interview at her company. Your barber may have a client who also happens to be a recruiter at the employer of your dreams.

The fascinating thing about a professional network is that it's boundless. Your network encompasses the contacts you know, but it may also encompass the people your contacts know, and so on. One employee based in Washington, D.C., revealed that the person who helped him find his current job was not even an acquaintance. "I wound up finding out about the opening through a good friend's girl-friend's aunt," he says. "The aunt got me in for the interview. My résumé was one of probably hundreds or certainly tens sitting on a pile. This woman went in to the president of the company and said, 'You have this open position and this person is applying for it. You really should look at him.' As I understand it, the president, in turn, went to HR and said that they should interview me."

The moral of that story is that you never know who might help you in your career. It's best to stay open-minded and to strive to main-tain and even broaden your network. This doesn't mean that you have to alter your life dramatically. Even simple changes can help to make networking a natural and even enjoyable part of your day. For one em-ployee at a nonprofit, that means sending e-mails to all his work con-tacts every so often in order "to catch up, to say 'hello,' to let them know that I'm thinking of them." For a director at global investment bank it means taking the time to socialize with past and present con-tacts, if even for a quick drink at a bar after work. "I always send Christmas cards," proclaims an administrative assistant at a health care insurance company. "That way all the people in my life—even friends I made years ago who now live quite a distance away—know that they're still on my radar."

In all of these instances networking is not divorced from regular life, but instead, integrated in a way that is satisfying both personally and professionally. Those who are more social and effusive may have an easier time networking than those who are naturally introverted. But even for the shy folks among us, networking doesn't have to be a forced affair, nor does it have to imply "social climbing." The plain fact of the matter is that networking is a win-win situation.

Melissa Walker, an alumna of Vassar College, underscores this notion. She says that she enjoys meeting with new graduates, telling them about her job in journalism, and giving them tips on how they might enter into the industry. "I love doing that—meeting with people, telling them my experiences. I love saying, 'Hey, this editorial assistant just left. You should send in your résumé for the position before it's advertised.'" Why—in addition to altruism—does she give so freely of her time? "Networking always benefits both parties," she explains. "Who knows, maybe the person [I help now] will be assigning articles in the future."

Walker's point—that networking works both ways—should quell fears that by calling people and asking them for information or advice, you must also sacrifice your pride. The truth is, many people are inclined to help someone who is thoughtful, polite, and professional in her inquiry. They are even happy to do it, especially if the person is truly eager to hear what they have to say. Dale Carnegie, the well-known author of *How to Win Friends & Influence People*, writes, "I never forgot that to be genuinely interested in other people is a most important quality for a salesperson to possess—for any person, for that matter."

That's not to say that asking people for help always works. But if you reach out to enough people, and you are generous in your approach, you will eventually find at least one person who will share valuable information and perhaps even offer a couple of employment leads.

The secret to successful networking is in your approach. Striking the right tone is critical. If you approach someone in a demanding way, as if you are entitled to be helped, then chances are you'll get nothing in return. Similarly, if you take a groveling, whiny, or self-pitying approach, you probably won't go far. So, just how do you strike the right tone? Sometimes a good litmus test is to ask yourself how would you react if someone approached you. What would it take for you to offer your thoughts and guidance? What would the person have to say and how would he have to phrase it? Would you be more comfortable if the person e-mailed you, or would you prefer a phone call or face-to-face communication?

As you begin to network, or to extend your existing network, it helps to know a little about the individuals you are approaching, including their career interests, or professional backgrounds, or hobbies, or where they went to school. Establishing commonality of interest may help to ease the passage from casual conversation to more pertinent "shop talk." Manager David Wittenberg explains that knowing something about a person's personality may also help to build a rapport. "Some people with certain personalities like to show off what they know. If you call them and say, 'I understand you are very good with this, or an expert at that,' they may respond positively. Others can't resist teaching. You might say, 'I understand you know a lot about this field. Would you be willing to explain such-and-such to me?' Yet another approach might be to see who's written articles in technical journals. A person might have published a presentation within his field, and he might be flattered—just tickled pink—to know that somebody on the outside has paid attention to his publication."

Of course, the people who are most easy to network with are the people with whom you already have ready-made connections. Below, in "Nine Ways to Network," you'll learn how to capitalize on the networking opportunities that are available to just about everyone. But ultimately, whether your network begins with a close-knit group of coworkers or a series of "cold calls," all that really matters is that you think of networking as a lifelong endeavor that will benefit other people as much as it will benefit you. Jordan Montminy, an Emmy Award–winning freelance film and TV editor, speaks of his own experience: "Ninety-eight percent of the time I find jobs through contacts I've already established. These might include former employers, fellow employees, friends who work in the business, friends of friends, people from various and circuitous connections I've made over the years. It's a cliché, but it's who you know."

Nine Ways to Network

FAMILY MEMBERS

Who would have thought that networking can begin with your own family? It's true—your mother, sister, uncle, or third cousin twice removed may hold the key to a great job.

Leigh Wetzel had solid project management experience in technology as well as production manager experience in television. Despite her stellar credentials, she had a hard time landing a job, due to a dreary economy. Although she had sent out close to a thousand résumés, incorporated the aid of headhunters, and combed through online job boards, the interviews she had managed to land had not taken her far.

She explains that she was at the end of her unemployment benefits and beginning to despair when she realized a tremendous opportunity was right under her nose. "I was out one day for lunch with a friend and saw an empty store space. I called my aunt, who is president of Paper Source (www.paper-source.com), and said, 'Why don't you open up a store here and let me manage it?' She responded, 'I was hoping you were calling me to help me sell products on our website.' I didn't think she realized how much work would go into making such a site. But I was interested. Eventually, her partner came out and interviewed me here in California and I was officially offered the position."

It might seem a no-brainer to approach family members about employment opportunities, but surprisingly, many people place an invisible barrier between their family life and their work life. While sometimes this barrier is necessary, just as often it becomes a needless obstacle on the way to fulfilling employment.

Even if don't think your relatives will be of much help, take the time to communicate with them about your employment needs and goals. You might find that someone in your family is a great sounding board, offering a sympathetic ear, smart advice, or even a contact that will put your job search on a better course. A senior teller at a bank who had recently been laid off was surprised to learn that his mother, a college professor, had a valuable contact in her own network. The mother, who walked her dog every morning in a public park, had become friendly with a fellow dog owner: an executive at Bank of America.

FRIENDS AND THEIR FRIENDS

Friendships are often built on common interests and values. Often, these interests and values extend to the working world, which is the reason that communicating with your friends about work-related issues can be of benefit. If you're looking for a new job, or thinking seriously about beginning a job search, it's a good idea to share this information with your friends. Like family, friends can give you the extra support and help you might need. Plus, because they know you and care about you, your friends will keep their eyes and ears open for opportunities that might match your qualifications. Many will go the extra mile to help you—something you can't expect acquaintances to do.

Even if a friend can't help you directly, he or she may have another friend who can. An indirect referral is better than no referral at all. In fact, once source estimates that a referred candidate is 75 percent more likely to be asked for an interview than a candidate who is completely unknown. A great way to expand your network is to meet these friends of friends. Be proactive in your approach. Throw a potluck dinner or a cocktail party and ask every invitee to bring someone else they know. Or, the next time you go out to eat or to the movies with a group, ask each person to invite at least one other.

Says recruiting expert Beth Camp: "The best way to get your hooks into a company is to join a friend who works at that company and is going out for drinks with his coworkers after work. That way you can meet his coworkers. You will start talking shop naturally and they will find out what you know and don't know. . . . This kind of specific networking really pays off." It does. After all, the more people you know, and the broader your network becomes, the better your chances for landing an interview.

SCHOOL ALUMNI

Some would argue that the most important aspect of college or graduate school is not the classes you take, or the information you learn, or the degree you get to take home. They would say that the real boon of being an alumnus/alumna is that you automatically enter into a network of people who can help you in your career.

One recent MBA graduate says a large part of his decision to attend business school was to network with other people in his field. He explains that the value of this networking might not be immediate, but it may become indispensable later on. "I think the value will be seen five or ten years down the line," he explains. "Ten years from now a friend I had in school might be a VP at one company and I might be a VP at another company, and at that point networking will have more meaning."

Other graduates see the fruits of their academic networking sooner rather than later. Jordan Montminy, a graduate of New York University, says that he has stayed in touch with those students who share his professional interests. "We end up recommending one another for jobs," he reveals.

Your school doesn't necessarily have to have name-brand value when it comes to student and alumni networking. In fact, some graduates of lesser-known institutions are even more eager to help old classmates than those who graduated from more recognized schools. One professional in human resources consulting, who had seen his university slip in the rankings, said that he frequently reaches out to new graduates because helping them to succeed also helps to "put a positive spotlight" on his school.

Even if you've graduated from school without contacts in your field of work, it's not too late to start building an alumni-based network. Most schools have an alumni association that students can use as a resource. Good alumni associations track where graduates are working year to year, and many actually encourage graduates to contact one another regarding employment opportunities. A trip to your school, or even a phone call or an e-mail to the alumni office, may provide you with the names and contact information of alumni working at some of your prospective companies. After that, it's up to you to strike up a conversation. But remember, you have a common connection on which to build a rapport: your alma mater.

PROFESSIONAL ORGANIZATIONS AND ASSOCIATIONS

Belonging to a professional or trade organization or association is another way to build your professional network. A senior graphic designer at a major automotive club believes her membership to local and national designers' groups has enabled her to meet professionals she wouldn't have come into contact with otherwise. She says attendance at the annual conferences, in particular, is a personal "must" for career-building. "It's a huge networking fest," she emphasizes. "Plus, you see a number of the most successful people in your field."

One student who is working toward an advanced degree in library science joined several library science organizations so that by the time she graduated, she would already have contacts in her field. "I joined one state chapter, one national chapter, and one chapter for minorities," she says. "So far, it has really paid off. Every week I receive a list of job openings through being on a listserv [an automatic online mailing list]." She goes on to say that she has met "five or six promising contacts online" over the span of only a few months.

The library science student underscores the point that all networking doesn't have to be face to face, although that is often the most effective way to communicate with people. Communicating with people via e-mail can work just as well, especially if you share something in common, such as membership to the same organization or experience in the same industry. Says associate editor Melissa Walker: "Most of the people I network with I've never met. It's all through e-mail at first—I usually do meet them in person later. Since I do a lot of reporting, I send many calls out for stories to magazine people and regular women, and a lot of people are just friendly. They're eager to help."

COWORKERS, PAST AND PRESENT

If you've been in the working world for any length of time, even in a summer job or an internship, you've undoubtedly met people who might be valuable to have in your network. It pays to keep in touch with these coworkers, even after you leave the job. After all, it's impossible to predict who might be able to help you ten months or even ten years down the line. Even if a coworker is in a different job capacity—perhaps you're in sales and he's in accounting—don't sever your ties. That person could have contacts at other companies who might be of assistance.

If you're presently working, a good way to strengthen your network is to think beyond your immediate department. Don't miss out on company-sponsored outings, which are a great way to get to know many different employees. Take the time to mingle with people in other departments at the coffee machine or the water cooler. When you're taking your lunch break, ask another coworker to join you, especially someone you don't know particularly well. You just might spark a friendship.

When you leave an employer, be sure to give your contact information to all the people you want to stay in touch with. Accept invitations to social events and extend such invitations yourself. Because it's easy to lose track of colleagues over time, put up reminders to check in with people every month or two. A well-placed Post-it or a note in your calendar can work wonders.

POLITICAL, SOCIAL, AND RELIGIOUS AFFILIATIONS

People find friends and even spouses though political, social, or religious affiliations, so why not find a job? If you're a member of any organization—a garden club, a social board committee, a political union, a church, a synagogue—don't be shy about chatting with people and telling them a little about yourself. You don't have to cite your career goals up front if the situation isn't right, but eventually, you can steer conversation toward this topic.

If you're in school, consider joining one or more clubs and activities. You don't necessarily have to join the basketball team if you've never dribbled a ball before. There are always organizations that welcome members with little or no experience, and organizations that don't require much of a commitment. At Thunderbird, the American Graduate School of International Management, for example, a group of students gather regularly for the "Eat Club." The only purpose of the club is for members to eat out at various restaurants in the area. Of course, if you're in interested in a job in marketing, for example, joining the marketing club makes sense. If no such club exists, consider starting one yourself.

Once you join an organization and actively participate in it, you may meet one or more members with whom you feel a growing kinship. Be sure to capitalize on this bond. Spending additional time with the people with whom you most easily relate is a sure way to bolster your network.

NEIGHBORS

There is probably no more convenient way to network than to call on someone who lives in the apartment next to yours or in the house down the street. Because neighbors come into contact with one another so frequently, it's only right to include them in the networking process. If you don't know your neighbors very well, networking is the perfect excuse to invite them over for a cup of coffee or to throw a neighbors-only shindig.

Neighbors are convenient to network with, but they're also valuable because they live locally and may know of opportunities that exist in and around your particular town or city. If you're sniffing around for a new position, let your neighbors know you're looking. Doing so over the phone is one way. But inviting your neighbors over for coffee and cookies is a surer way of winning them over.

CAREER FAIRS

A career fair is an event that lasts a day or more and that enables a sizable number of employers to mingle with a sizable number of students or jobseekers. True to its name, a career fair often has a lively, social atmosphere, where people are encouraged to exchange business cards, ask and field questions, and discuss employment opportunities. Career fairs are frequently held on college and graduate school campuses, but many are also thrown for professionals who are already in the working world. Career fairs are always advertised, so be sure to check your local newspaper for upcoming events.

Despite the fun atmosphere many career fairs foster, they are in essence serious business events that require candidates to visit the companies' promotional booths, drop off their résumés, discuss their work experience, and generally attract the interest of company representatives. The hiring managers and recruiters at various company booths may even hold impromptu interviews with promising candidates, so it's imperative for everyone to be at their best.

There aren't many opportunities for jobseekers to come face to face with the people who have true hiring power, so career fairs are extremely important for this reason alone. Before you attend a career fair, be sure to have your affairs in order. If this is your first career fair, ask people who have already attended some to give you pointers on what you can expect. Dress professionally, bring at least a dozen copies of your résumé, have answers ready to the questions you may be asked, and be prepared to ask some questions of your own (see chapter 7, "Preparing for the Almighty Interview"). If you know the companies that will be present at the fair, spend some time researching which you would like to target. Often, there aren't enough hours to visit all the booths—so be diligent about how you spend your time. After you speak with a company representative, jot down notes about what you discussed, and don't forget to ask for a business card. If your talk went well, you'll want to follow up.

An added bonus of career fairs: Employers frequently bring little freebies emblazoned with the company logo, such as T-shirts, pens, calendars, calculators, mugs, and candy. Even if you don't land an interview, chances are you won't leave empty-handed!

COLD CALLING

It sounds a little like a telephone on ice, but the cold call is actually an important tool of networking. Cold calling is calling a person or business without prior contact in order to inquire about employment opportunities. For many, the idea of cold calling is chilling. Dialing up a complete stranger doesn't seem like a logical way to carry out a job search. Yet when done correctly, a cold call can showcase some important professional traits, including resilience, determination, and interpersonal skills. In the best-case scenario, it can also lead to an interview.

Cold calling is a salesman's device. The premise is that the more people you contact, the better your chances of scoring a deal. In a way salesmanship is integrally connected to the job search, only instead of selling a product or service, you're selling yourself. Specifically, you're selling the notion that you would be a valuable addition to a company's team. And therein lies the key to the cold call. When you pick up the phone, you must think of yourself not as a nervous jobseeker eager for a lead, but rather, as a confident professional who has the qualifications that would benefit an employer.

How do you make this leap? It's not easy, admits one woman in retail who had taken off several years to raise two children and wanted to rejoin the workforce. She admits the cold call took some practice. "I was much smoother on my eighth or ninth attempt than I was on my first. . . . I called up many businesses, and the majority of them didn't take more than fifteen seconds to decide they weren't interested. Finally, I caught one man who asked me where I'd gone to school. As it happened, we'd gone to the same college. He took a liking to me after that. I was asked in for an interview the following week."

This woman's example shows that it helps to make a connection with the person you are cold calling. However, this is not always possible. The plain truth about cold calling is that the failure rate is high. Yet the rewards can be great if you encounter even one person who recognizes your potential. Below are some techniques for making the cold call a little warmer.

✦ Write a script for your cold call, outlining one or two of your most valuable Key Selling Points (see chapter 7). Remember that you are trying to impress the person on the other end of the line. Modify your script so that these selling points are in sync with each company's specific needs. A customized delivery is crucial.

✦ Be clear on your goals and what you have to offer. Nothing will turn off an employer faster than a person who is not clear about his objectives.

✦ Introduce yourself in a way that will spark interest. Saying your name immediately followed by your area of expertise might do the trick.

✦ Work on your voice—make sure you sound professional, sharp, and cheerful, but never insincere or calculating. It helps to practice both your voice and your script on a trusted friend who can offer you feedback and suggestions.

◆   Figure out who is on the other end of the line. Receptionists and other gatekeepers will usually pick up the phone before hiring managers will. Be prepared to answer gatekeeper-type questions such as "What is the reason for your call?" and "What company are you with?" A confident answer and an assured tone might allow you to pass through this initial screen. No matter who picks up the phone, be professional. Treat everyone with equal courtesy and respect.

◆   Use the "rule of three." If you've tried calling three times, or left up to three messages with no response, throw in the towel. Calling any more than that will only irritate the person you are trying to reach. Says a senior human resources consultant with a well-known mutual insurance company: "Candidates can call me and leave a voicemail message, but it's hard for me to do callbacks due to the volume of calls I receive." She goes on to say she does follow up with many people who leave inquiries, but that repeat messages "are more burden than value."

◆   Substitute your e-mail account for your phone. These days many businesspeople are more apt to answer e-mails than voicemail messages anyway. E-mailing requires less effort on both ends because people don't need to think and speak on the fly; they can actually take the time to word their correspondence carefully. If you're better at written communication than you are at oral communication, consider sending "cold e-mails" rather than making cold calls. In this case, though, you'll need to address your e-mail to a single person. Consider calling the company gatekeeper, who may be more inclined to pass along the e-mail address of the hiring manager than the phone number. Blindly e-mailing a company at a general address can pretty much guarantee a lack of results—unless the company happens to be very small. For more tips on e-mailing, see "The Unspoken Rules of Online Job Correspondence" in Chapter Six.

+ Keep track of your phone calls. If you leave a message, you'll want to know the name and title of the person who is returning your call and what information you've already provided.

+ Be prepared for standard responses from human resources personnel and other hiring managers. You will probably receive some brush-off responses like, "The only thing you can do is send your résumé to our HR department," or even, "We are not currently hiring." However, some responses will allow you more opportunity to sell yourself. Be prepared to sell yourself if you hear a question such as "What kind of experience do you have?" or "What attracts you to our company?"

+ Don't become discouraged. Cold calling isn't easy, and a few hang-ups can make even the most stalwart person question himself. Take breaks and keep in mind that the process isn't personal.

+ Remember that your ultimate goal is to get an interview. To that end, if you do speak with someone who has hiring power and if you establish a rapport with that person, ask outright if you can come in for an interview. The question might seem presumptuous, but it's been known to work.

More Tips on Networking

+ *Call or e-mail your networking contacts regularly.* This is especially important during periods when their guidance or support is not necessary. If you contact a person only during times of need, he or she may feel put upon or even used. Conversely, regular communication, in good times and bad, can only bolster the foundation of a relationship. A former vice-president of a major health insurance company says that he appreciated when people he'd helped out over the years "called me to let me know how they were doing." He goes on to say that he "would not be inclined to help someone more than once if they didn't express their appreciation the first time." Remembering people on their birthdays or other special occasions is a good way to make contacts feel welcome and wanted in your life.

✦ *Be a friend to others.* Always remember that networking is a two-way street. If someone asks for your help—and this help is within reason—give it with a smile. You'll feel like a better person for doing so. At the same time, you'll put yourself in a favorable position when it comes time for you to ask a favor. In fact, the best networker is one who offers to help without ever being asked.

✦ *Remember names.* It sounds simple, but remembering someone's name can make an indelibly positive impression on that person. Remembering someone's name is actually to pay her a compliment, for it means that you have committed her to memory. On the other hand, not remembering a person's name or mispronouncing it is akin to a subtle insult. Everyone has been in this situation. You meet someone, introduce yourself, and five minutes later, you hear, "What was your name again?" The very question can make you feel small and forgettable. On the other hand, hearing your name in conversation—"Can you tell me more about your business plan, Jessie?" or "Ming, I really enjoyed that speech you gave"—may lift your spirits. In networking, a special and concerted effort to remember names is important, for it sets you apart as a considerate and personable contact. For tips on remembering names, see "Real-Life Interview Mishaps (and What You Can Learn from Them)" in chapter 8.

✦ *Use the names of the people who refer you.* As you network, one or more of your contacts may refer you to a person at a company of interest to you. When you speak to the person at that company, don't forget to mention that so-and-so referred you. The fact that you were referred by a mutual acquaintance or friend may take you a lot farther than if there were no common ground.

◆ *Respect limitations on people's time.* As you network keep in mind that the job search may be a higher priority for you than it is for others. If a contact agrees to help you, give that person a bit of leeway in terms of time. One human resources manager at an international IT provider agreed to assist a jobseeker who was a friend of a friend. However, that jobseeker quickly took advantage of the manager's goodwill gesture. "I was willing to put in some effort and time into helping this candidate on his job search," the human resources professional reveals. "[But] he followed up with many e-mails, and then a phone call, and it almost started to become bothersome. My advice to an overly persistent jobseeker is to make sure the person has received your message, then lay low."

◆ *Pass out your business card.* It's not always convenient or wise to pass out your résumé at every networking function you attend. An easier way to make sure that people remember you is to keep a stack of business cards in your pocket or purse. When you meet a person who might become a professional contact, don't hesitate to dole out your card. Obviously, if you're between jobs, you don't want to give a business card bearing the name of your former employer. In this case, consider investing in cards that list only your name, contact information, professional title, and/or area of expertise. Many printing companies—including chain stores like Kinko's—can turn around a simple, professional-looking, and inexpensive card in a matter of days.

◆ *Create a thirty-second "commercial."* If you've already prepared a script for cold calling, then you're well on your way to making a thirty-second "commercial." Like the cold call script, the thirty-second "commercial" is an opportunity for you to promote yourself and your qualifications in a way that is concise and compelling. It is a useful networking tool because when you meet another person for the first time, you inevitably reveal bits of information about yourself. You might as well make sure those bits of information reflect your career aspirations.

When creating your commercial, start with your name, then add a line or two about your area of expertise, or a particular skill or achievement. The following is an example of a commercial from a person in business school: "I just started an MBA program at Rutgers University. Prior to my studies, I was a junior compensation analyst at Unilever for three years. I worked with human resources on analyzing and adjusting salary levels for positions throughout the organization. Now I'm keeping an eye open for senior compensation analyst jobs in or around New Jersey for when I graduate."

NOTE: Obviously, the content of the thirty-second commercial is entirely up to you. When to use your commercial—and when to abstain—is also your choice. In some networking situations, such as career fairs, jumping right in with your commercial is usually a good idea. However, in other situations you will have to exercise discretion as to whether you should start with your commercial right away or wait for a more appropriate opportunity.

✦ *Ask your contacts for contacts.* In networking, speaking with people is a little like rooting for truffles. You may have to dig around a bit before you find a nugget that is valuable. Often times you will network with someone who knows little about your profession. Yet he or she may know another person who works at a company that is on your Prospective Employer List. For this reason, you should never hesitate to ask your contacts the fateful question: "Do you know anyone who works in my industry?"

If the answer is "Yes," why not pursue the lead? Ask where that person works and what her position is. Ask if that person would be amenable to speaking with you about job opportunities. Ask if you can have that person's phone number or e-mail address, and if you can say that you were referred. Listen carefully to the information that is given to you and jot down the important parts, especially names and contact information. And don't wait too long to follow up.

The Informational Interview

While informational interviews are primarily organized for the purpose of information-gathering, they can also lead to job interviews. In fact, most jobseekers have two agendas when soliciting informational interviews: collecting general information about the industry and/or company, and finding out about specific job opportunities. So, on an informational interview is it all right to declare both intentions?

The answer is a resounding "No!" The fact is, it's plain rude to ask a person for an informational interview, only to spring the job question without notice. Unlike the cold call, where the person answering the phone is caught off-guard, the informational interviewer has already set aside time in her schedule to meet with you. She's already shown generosity and kindness in agreeing to answer your questions. Therefore, to ask for a job is actually to mislead your interviewer and to inspire feelings of mistrust. Says the director of a global investment bank, "If the informational interviewer has a job that's available, they probably will offer it to you anyway. If they don't have a job—don't ask for it. Say 'Thank you,' be done with it, and stay in touch. Always stay in touch, because that person may think of you later on when a job does become available."

If you go on an informational interview in the hope of landing a job interview, but aren't allowed to ask for one, what then are you supposed to do? "Walk a tightrope," declares one jobseeker in the pharmaceuticals industry who has been on four informational interviews since being laid off. "Whoever is interviewing you will probably ask you about your job status. When you say you're looking, you're also tacitly asking for help. So indirectly, you're expressing your desire for a job interview, even though you would never dare ask directly."

In the informational interview, then, diplomacy and tactfulness are valuable. What you're really trying to do is to take a back-door approach to finding a job by presenting your skills and qualifications to the informational interviewer, and then letting her decide how to proceed. It's very possible that your interview will go no farther than a one-time meeting. However, if you impress your interviewer—and if there is in fact a job opening that matches your qualifications—you may be able to parlay the initial meeting into something much greater. Here are suggestions on how to do just that.

✦ Be specific about how much time you need. The informational interview should be brief and at a time convenient for your interviewer. Asking for twenty to thirty minutes is a good benchmark. Remember, your interviewer may have other commitments, so be respectful of her schedule.

✦ Learn as much as you can beforehand about the company where your informational interviewer works. Presumably the company is already on your Prospective Employer List. If it's not, then use the research techniques introduced in Chapter Two to brush up.

✦ Map out what you want to cover. Prior to the interview, come up with a list of questions that have not already been answered by your research. Keep in mind that the interview will be brief, so you will have to separate the questions that you need answered from those that are less pressing.

✦ Be a good listener. The informational interview requires a dialogue—not a soliloquy. Asking thoughtful and intelligent questions, taking notes, showing sincere interest, and giving your interviewer ample time to speak is much better than monopolizing the conversation with a string of questions.

+ Be ready to answer questions about yourself. Naturally, your interviewer will want to know a little about you. Your thirty-second "commercial" may be useful during an informational interview. Don't forget to bring along at least one copy of your résumé in case your interviewer asks to see it.

+ Be yourself. You may find yourself nervous, flustered, and shy— it's only natural to feel a little unnatural in an interview setting. Take a deep breath and make every effort to communicate your true personality to your informational interviewer. Helping her to feel comfortable in your presence can only help your cause.

Ultimately, the same rules of etiquette apply to the informational interview as they do to the job interview. You should call the day before to confirm, show up on time, dress professionally, and send a thank-you note when your interview is over. You shouldn't enter the informational interview angling for a job interview, but keeping the idea in the back of your mind doesn't hurt. Says Manager David Wittenberg: "The important thing is not to come across as a 'taker'—someone who only wants a job. If you've been able to build a rapport and to create value for the other person, then it can be appropriate to mention your situation." For more detailed interviewing tips, see Chapter Seven.

Key Chapter Points

+ Building and drawing upon a professional network is absolutely essential to the job search. It's probably fair to say that for every person who finds a job through an online careers site, another ten find employment through people they know.

+ Networking is a long-term process that ultimately benefits everyone involved.

✦ Networking requires regular communication with groups of people from different areas of your life. Nine ways to network include family members, friends and their friends, school alumni, professional organizations and associations, past and present coworkers, neighbors, career fair opportunities, "cold call" techniques, and members of political, social, and religious organizations.

✦ Cold calling is calling a person or business without prior contact in order to inquire about employment opportunities. Although the cold call has a high rate of failure, even one successful phone conversation can pave the way to a job interview.

✦ Although the informational interview is arranged for the purpose of information-gathering, it can in some cases lead to employment opportunities.

Chapter Four

YOUR RÉSUMÉ: THE BREAD AND BUTTER OF ANY JOB SEARCH

The résumé is a reflection of your professional persona. It is a preview of what you have to offer an employer. And perhaps most importantly, it is a marketing tool used to lure hiring managers. Because the résumé is all these things and more, creating one—or improving upon an older version—is not a task to be taken lightly.

The first thing to consider when beginning your résumé is what you are trying to achieve. Many people mistakenly believe that the best résumés are those that accurately summarize their previous professional experience. But in reality, the best résumés are those that get noticed by hiring managers—period. Everything about the résumé, from format, to font, to language, should be tailored toward that end.

In creating or updating a résumé, you should go back to your Personal Career Inventory. Here, you will already have listed much of the material needed for your résumé, including your educational background, skills, and industry experience. On just about any résumé, this information should be divvied up into various sections such as "Objective," "Professional Experience," "Skills and Training," and "Education."

The sequence of these sections—and certainly their contents—will depend upon what kind of background you have. However, in just about all cases, résumés follow reverse chronological order. That is, the experience you had most recently should be listed first, the second most recent experience second, and so on. A senior human resources manager with a mutual insurance company emphasizes that although a résumé should walk her through the important points of a candidate's work history, it shouldn't take her along a lengthy and arduous trail. A few "bullet [points don't] tell me enough, but a novel isn't helpful either," she says.

All résumés, too, must be clean and easy to read. A crowded format or an unusually small or hard-to-read font will only bring tears to a hiring manager's eyes—and those won't be tears of joy. "The readability and visibility of a résumé are important—there is no question," says a human resources manager in a federal judiciary. "Some people use every single spare space on the page. Nothing stands out. It doesn't look like a résumé—it looks like a page from James Joyce." This HR manager's point is well taken. A résumé that's easy on the eyes may also be the way to a hiring manager's heart. Consider who will be reading your résumé. Remember that the person who initially screens résumés at a company may do so day in and day out. He may very well look at hundreds, even thousands, of résumés every week. In all likelihood, this person won't spend any time on a cramped, marginless, or otherwise unattractive résumé.

All résumés must conform to standard length requirements. The challenge most people face with the résumé is space management. Some people don't believe a page or two is enough to outline all their professional achievements. Other people, especially those fresh out of school or with limited work experience, wonder how they'll possible fill all that white space. No matter who you are or how much work experience you have had, though, no résumé—with the possible exception of a résumé from a high-ranking executive with twenty-five plus years of experience—should exceed two pages. In fact, whenever possible, a résumé should be limited to only one. The reason is simple: hiring managers simply don't have the time to skim through a tome. They want the relevant information, and they want it fast. Says the mutual insurance company professional: "If I print [out] a résumé and it's five pages, I will only read the first two. Applicants have to consider and respect limits on a person's time. Don't say it in a page when you can say it in two paragraphs."

Résumé writing should have a businesslike tone. HR experts strongly advise jobseekers to avoid using sarcasm or humor. You don't know who will be reading your résumé or what their dispositions are like—so why take a risk?

Tips for Writing the Perfect Résumé

STYLE TIPS

No matter how you choose to lay out your résumé, be consistent. Use the same font, format, and grammatical techniques throughout. Don't stray below a ten-point font, as anything smaller is hard to read. Leave a margin of roughly one inch around the periphery of the page. Avoid personal pronouns, unnecessary articles, and general wordiness, especially in your experience section. For example, in terms of space-saving, it's better to say "Renegotiated long-term contracts with vendors, driving down the cost of business by an average of 23 percent" than "My duties included, but were not limited to, renegotiating long-term contracts with vendors, driving down the cost of business by between 21 and 25 percent, depending on the vendor."

Whenever possible, avoid using abbreviations. Use italics, bold, and all capital letters sparingly. The point of using these effects is emphasis, but there is such a thing as emphasis overkill. Use a combination of bulleted points and paragraphs to make the various sections of your résumé stand out. Using only one or the other will give your résumé a flat, homogenous look. Bear in mind that hiring managers at large companies receive so many résumés that they spend very little time on each—twenty or thirty seconds. Make your time count by making your most important information pop off the page.

A résumé written by hand or by typewriter may have worked fifty years ago, but it won't pass muster now. Today, résumés should be printed with black ink on high-quality white or ivory paper. Avoid gimmicks like unusually colored ink, paper in nontraditional sizes or shapes, or enclosing a photograph of yourself. "Stand out from the crowd, but remain professional," advises Robin Pelzman, a former human resources specialist at Hewlett-Packard. "Once, I got over 550 résumés for a technical writer position. The résumés I received were just over the top—colored paper, examples of fiction, etc. The résumé that stood out was creative, but professional, with a beautifully written cover letter. While the person's technical writing was not in the same industry, her experience and writing talents were still applicable. She distinguished herself by being on point, explaining and demonstrating what in her writing background was applicable to the position."

In other words, forgo tricks and stratagems, and instead showcase real skills and accomplishments.

NOTE: Candidates who work in a creative industry such as graphic design may deviate from the norm in terms of traditional résumé style, but only if an artistic slant is congruous with the prospective employer and position.

FORMATTING TIPS

How you format your résumé will depend on the job you are looking for, your professional background, and your personal sense of style. For example, someone with little work experience may opt to list his education section first, while someone who has been in the workforce for a few years may opt to move the education section to the bottom of the page.

While the chronological résumé is by far the most common template used by jobseekers, the skills-based résumé is preferred by some professionals, especially those who are entrepreneurs, shifting careers, or in trade-based profession. People who have used the same skills but in different industries may also opt for the skills-based résumé. The skills-based résumé emphasizes particular achievements or abilities, and it is functional rather than chronological. It allows the job-seeker to underscore aspects of his work history that are more relevant to the positions he is seeking. If you've held a number of different or unrelated jobs during a relatively short period of time and are worried about being labeled as a job-hopper, the skills-based résumé could be the answer for you. This format can also work well for those entering the workforce for the first time or after a long absence (such as recent grads with no prior formal work experience, stay-at-home moms or dads now seeking outside employment, or caregivers who have spent a year or more treating an ill or aging family member). It could also be a good choice if your prior work experience is more relevant to your target industry than what you're doing presently.

Despite the advantages of the skills-based résumé, many hiring managers profess to prefer the old-fashioned chronological résumé because of the structure and employment timeline it provides. One HR manager says, "Skills-based résumés are popular among people who have been out of work as parents and those who have had many jobs in a short period of time. But I still like to see a chronological résumé because I like to get the whole story [on a person's work history]." In other words, skip the skills-based résumé unless it seems absolutely necessary.

All résumés, regardless of format, should grab the reader's attention early, and thereafter provide information that is concise, precise, and in keeping with the requirements of each individual job posting. It's tempting to include every single skill you've ever performed on your résumé. But including too much information has its drawbacks. First, your résumé may become too long and cumbersome for the capricious eyes of hiring managers. And second, by including too much information, you may include some points that are simply not relevant.

Says Robin Pelzman: "Don't put everything you've ever done in your work life on your résumé, including details of entirely irrelevant jobs or work you did prior to your current career."

Deciding what to include and exclude will be contingent upon the components of the individual job listing. If a job calls for more computer skills than analytical skills, for instance, you may want to highlight the technical skills that you possess, and omit or downsize descriptions of your analytical skills. Of course, you should always include your name at the top of the page, followed by your address, phone number, e-mail address, Website address, and any other relevant contact information. Writing the word "résumé" or "curriculum vitae" (as the résumé is also called) is not necessary.

RÉSUMÉ SECTIONS

Major sections of the résumé are outlined below to give you some tips on how to catch a hiring manager's attention. For the purposes of this book, we're using one group of headings. But bear in mind that different people may choose to title their sections differently. For example, one person might write "Professional Experience," while another might write "Employment History," or "Experience and Accomplishments," or "Business Experience," or just plain "Experience" for the same section. There is not necessarily a right or wrong section heading. Use the heading that best reflects your own work experience.

OBJECTIVE

The objective consists of one or two lines at the top of your résumé, under your name and contact information. It should describe in detail what job you are trying to obtain.

Different hiring managers debate the necessity, and indeed the value, of the objective. If you are applying to a company that has more than one position that may fit your qualifications, it's often best to leave out the objective, as having it might disqualify you for certain jobs and ultimately limit your options. However, in a situation where you are pursuing only one job at a given company and have the exact job title and description on hand, you may use the objective to ensure that the hiring manager directs your résumé to the right place.

In lieu of an objective, you may also opt to use a summary of qualifications. A summary of qualifications is exactly what it sounds like: a brief listing of your key skills and experience. If you have an advanced degree or considerable work experience, the summary of qualifications may be your best option. It enables a hiring manager to know at a glance what the rest of your résumé contains.

EDUCATION

The education section of your résumé is something that most hiring managers notice. If you've attended a very prestigious school, are a recent graduate, or have a degree that is extremely relevant to a certain position, it's a good idea to put your education first so that the section draws the eye of the reader. Under education you should list, in reverse chronological order, the schools you've attended, years attended, graduation dates, grade point averages (GPAs), degrees, majors and minors, and any relevant awards or honors. The human resources manager at a federal judiciary stresses the importance of including graduation dates, in particular. "We can eliminate people who wrote they 'attended' school, which doesn't necessarily mean they graduated," he reveals. "HR people hate when people try to disguise the fact that they didn't graduate." He also advises jobseekers to include their GPAs, even if those aren't perfect. If a candidate doesn't include her GPA, hiring professionals will assume—rightly or wrongly—that it is shamefully low.

If you've been in the workplace for a few years or longer, putting your education lower on your résumé is not a bad option. Ones consultant explains why she decided to de-emphasize her MBA degree. "My résumé is that of a mid-level professional. I'm not a fresh MBA coming out," she says. "Instead of focusing on my education like most people in school did, I focused instead on my eight years of work experience.

I'm trying to show my MBA as a continuation of my professional experience rather than as a starting point to a more entry-level MBA job." Although her education was very solid, this consultant decided to put that section last on her résumé.

EXPERIENCE

Experience is often the most important section of any résumé, for it shows what a candidate has already accomplished, and thus, what she is capable of accomplishing in the future. The experience section should always include the names and locations of your employers, your dates of employment, job titles, and brief but measurable descriptions of your tasks.

A smart jobseeker will use the experience section not to tick off every job experience she's ever had, but those that best emphasize performance. To that end, it's essential not only to mention results, but also to quantify them. For example, Justin Moore, who formerly worked as a manager at an international travel agency, writes in his résumé that in three years he "increased the number of weekly group tour destinations from eight to fourteen, increasing seasonal quarterly revenue by U.S. $650,000." This description is infinitely more informative than simply saying he "increased the number of weekly group tour destinations." Quantifiable data is attractive because it is specific and it affirms the person's ability to achieve measurable results.

In constructing your experience section, it helps to think like an employer. What would an employer want to see? What information would be important and what information would be less important, or worse, potentially damaging? Says a graphic designer: "[In applying to jobs] I made sure to give relevant experience, not necessarily all my experience. Employers need a specific type of job done—they want to see work related to the kind of projects you will be doing on the job. You have to be on the same path as the employer, trying to reach the same goals." Indeed, if you list information that is different from the call of duty or if you appear overqualified, many employers will shy away from your résumé. Although you cannot change actual position titles or experience, you can prioritize the information, highlighting those aspects of your experience that are most applicable to each open position.

As mentioned earlier, it's not always necessary to list every job you've ever held. To keep your résumé concise, you may opt to list only your most recent positions or the last ten to fifteen years of your work history, whichever is shorter. If you're a new college graduate, jobs you held in high school may not be appropriate, so use your best judgment. What is most important is that your critical information is visible when the reader is skimming the page. To that end, it's usually best to use brief descriptions rather than lengthy sentences.

If you have a long work history, but believe that your former titles and company names are relevant to a position you are seeking, Robin Pelzman suggests to "list them as 'previous experience' and do it by year, job title and company only, and that's just so you don't have years 'missing' from your résumé. If the content of those jobs is irrelevant to your current search, omit it. However, don't shy away from listing relevant skills and experience even if the job where you got that experience isn't in the same field."

SKILLS

The skills section of the résumé has varying degrees of importance. For people in technical fields, it can be the most important aspect of the résumé. But for other professionals, skills may be somewhat less important than experience.

Include in your skills section technical skills, language skills, certifications, and any other accomplishments or areas of expertise that may be relevant to the position for which you are applying. Beware of including outdated skills, however. Especially in the field of technology, certain programming languages expire fast—and you don't want to be touting a skill that is no longer viable.

There are two valid schools of thought on how to prioritize your listings in the skills section. The first says you should list your skills in order of importance to the specific hiring manager. For a job that requires fluency in German, for example, you'll want to include fluency in this language at the beginning. The other school of thought, however, says that you should list your skills in order of proficiency. If you're an expert at using Microsoft Excel, for example, you might list this skill first, followed by other skills that you know well but haven't quite mastered.

ACTIVITIES

Not all jobseekers will necessarily have an activities section. But if you're a new graduate, the activities section may be an important part of your résumé. If you haven't had much work experience, your activities—membership to clubs, organizations, sports teams, etc.—will give potential employers a sense of what is important to you and where you've dedicated your time and energy. Keep in mind that some activities are more pertinent than others. Membership to a soccer league, for example, shows that you are a team player—a fact that may be relevant to a company. But beware of listing an activity that doesn't have any bearing on your suitability for a job.

AWARDS, HONORS, AND AFFILIATIONS

Awards or accolades you've earned, or titles that have been bestowed upon you, may demonstrate to prospective employers your potential for leadership. If an award or honor is pertinent to your field of expertise, consider listing it on your résumé. Also, consider listing your professional affiliations, especially if they are recognizable to potential employers.

TAILOR YOUR RÉSUMÉ

It's impossible to underestimate the importance of tailoring your résumé, or tweaking your information so that it targets each individual job opening. Indeed, sending the same version of your résumé to every company is likely to diminish your chances of getting job interviews.

While you can't change job titles or in any way deceive your reader, you can rearrange your information so that it is targeted. Says Robin Pelzman: "Tailor your objective. Tailor your accomplishments listed under your experience. Take the cues that are in the ad and tailor without altering your actual experience."

Your Prospective Employer List will come in handy as you tweak and refine. In tailoring your résumé for a company, look not only at the job advertisement, but also at the information you've collected independently and, if applicable, on an informational interview. Use employee profiles, news on services or product lines, or whatever other information appears relevant to the process of customizing your résumé.

THE LANGUAGE OF YOUR RÉSUMÉ

Dynamic and vivid language on your résumé is one way to capture the attention of hiring managers. In describing your employment experience, in particular, you will want to use language that in and of itself evokes professionalism, aptitude, and strength. The most effective way to capitalize on language is to use action verbs. For example, one jobseeker rephrased for the better a bulleted point under his most recent job title. Instead of writing "made changes in approach to external consulting projects," he wrote, "designed, implemented, and executed changes in approach to external consulting projects." Doesn't that sound more impressive? That's the point! Verbs that connote authority and competence simply read better.

The following is a list of action verbs that may come in handy as you refine the language of your résumé.

Action Verbs

accelerated	authored	coached	coordinated
accomplished	authorized	collaborated	corrected
achieved	automated	collected	corresponded
acquainted	awarded	combined	counseled
adapted	balanced	commissioned	created
administered	benchmarked	communicated	cultivated
advanced	brainstormed	compiled	decreased
aided	broadened	completed	defined
allocated	budgeted	composed	delegated
amplified	built	computed	delivered
analyzed	calculated	conceived	demonstrated
anticipated	canvassed	conceptualized	described
appraised	capitalized	condensed	designated
arranged	cataloged	conducted	designed
ascertained	centralized	conferred	detected
assembled	chaired	consolidated	determined
assessed	challenged	constructed	developed
assigned	championed	consulted	devised
assisted	channeled	contacted	devoted
attained	charted	contrasted	directed
attended	checked	contributed	discovered
audited	clarified	controlled	dispatched
augmented	classified	converted	displayed

disseminated	explained	helped	involved
distinguished	extended	hired	joined
distributed	facilitated	honed	judged
diversified	familiarized	hosted	juxtaposed
documented	fielded	identified	launched
doubled	financed	illuminated	lectured
edited	focused	illustrated	led
effected	forecasted	implemented	litigated
elected	forged	improved	lobbied
eliminated	formalized	increased	located
employed	formed	induced	maintained
enabled	formulated	influenced	managed
endorsed	fortified	informed	mapped
enforced	fostered	initiated	marketed
engaged	founded	innovated	maximized
enhanced	fulfilled	inspected	measured
enriched	functioned	inspired	mediated
established	gained	instituted	mentored
estimated	gathered	instructed	met
evaluated	gauged	insured	minimized
examined	generated	interfaced	moderated
exceeded	granted	interpreted	modified
executed	grouped	interviewed	monitored
exercised	guided	introduced	motivated
expanded	handled	invented	narrated
expedited	headed	invested	navigated

negotiated	presided	reduced	saved
netted	prevented	referred	scheduled
nurtured	processed	refined	screened
observed	procured	regulated	secured
obtained	produced	reinforced	selected
offered	programmed	remedied	served
offset	projected	remodeled	serviced
operated	promoted	reorganized	settled
orchestrated	proposed	repaired	shaped
ordered	provided	replaced	shortened
organized	publicized	reported	showed
oriented	published	represented	signed
originated	pursued	requested	simplified
overhauled	qualified	researched	solved
oversaw	quantified	resolved	spearheaded
participated	quoted	responded	specified
patented	raised	restored	sponsored
performed	ranked	restructured	stabilized
persuaded	rated	retained	staffed
phased	received	retrieved	standardized
pinpointed	recommended	revamped	started
pioneered	reconciled	reversed	steered
placed	recorded	reviewed	stimulated
planned	recovered	revised	strategized
prepared	recruited	revitalized	streamlined
presented	rectified	safeguarded	strengthened

structured	synchronized	transported	valued
studied	synthesized	treated	verbalized
submitted	systematized	trimmed	verified
substantiated	tailored	tripled	vitalized
substituted	targeted	undertook	volunteered
suggested	taught	underwent	welcomed
summarized	tested	unified	widened
supervised	tightened	united	won
supplied	trained	updated	worked
supported	transferred	upgraded	wrote
surpassed	transformed	utilized	
surveyed	translated	validated	

Résumé "Dos" and "Don'ts"

DO USE A SPELL CHECKER

According to many human resources experts, some of the most common résumé errors are a result of not using a spell checker, which is an application within most word processing programs that looks for spelling errors. They emphasize again and again that even one typo on a résumé may be grounds for dismissing a candidate. One professional, Kathleen Pierce, experienced this situation firsthand. She says, "I realized after two weeks of having my résumé up on online job boards, I had a typo. No wonder I didn't hear from any employers."

Although correct spelling is important, it simply isn't enough when it comes to résumés. Says HR expert Robin Pelzman: "The most basic of all advice is that spell-check doesn't pick up all [spelling and grammatical] errors. People cannot and should not rely on it for their cover letters and résumés. Doing so shows a lack of effort and a lack of attention to detail—not positive signs for an attentive HR professional." Indeed, even after using a spell checker, it helps to have at least one skilled reader double-check your résumé for proper sentence structure and punctuation. Pierce agrees. "Check, double-check, and have a friend triple-check," she says.

DO MAKE YOUR RÉSUMÉ SCANNABLE

Nowadays, many companies scan their incoming résumés electronically, especially if those résumés are being submitted into an online database. Scanning allows companies to search through all résumés they've received for specific information. Explains Robin Pelzman: "Years ago, we scanned in every résumé and cover letter we received, and then we would search by keywords like 'Linux' or 'C++' or previous employment at 'IBM' or 'Compaq.' We would do an initial run and then sort from there. I'm sure the technology is even more sophisticated now, so people should make sure the language and terminology on their résumés is current, not out-of-date." While some hiring managers frown upon using jargon, or words that are in vogue one moment and out of style the next, they do endorse the use of language that is current and industry-specific, and they admit that this kind of language may be part of a keyword search.

There is no way to guarantee that your résumé will be scannable by every company, as different employers use different hardware and software to sift through résumés. The best way to find out how to format your résumé is actually to call each company's human resources department and inquire about résumé scanning guidelines. If such guidelines are unavailable, you can still take basic steps to maximize your résumé's scannability. First and foremost, think simple. Use a common font like Times New Roman or Arial, and make sure the individual letters don't touch each other (scanners won't be able to differentiate these letters—or characters, as they are also called). If you use a slash mark

(/) or a dash (—), insert a space before and after it to avoid letter blending. If you're mailing your résumé via regular mail, avoid folding your résumé or using staples. Both staples and creases may present problems for a scanner.

DON'T FUDGE YOUR RÉSUMÉ

Telling the truth on your résumé may seem like a given, but thousands of candidates are eliminated for jobs each year because of false information. With thorough background checks a requirement of many companies, there's little chance of slipping under the radar with lies big or small. Common offenses include inaccurate dates of employment and graduation, and falsified information regarding undergraduate and graduate degrees. Says a consultant at a global consulting firm who places senior-level candidates: "People at the executive level need to be extra prepared to have their lives be an open book." Indeed, candidates at any level may be exposed to a fairly detailed background search. In fact, one source at a background-check company says that "10 to 15 percent of all candidates" have either hidden or falsified information.

An HR expert at a federal judiciary explains that some people try to hide how long they've been out of school for various reasons, such as a fear of age discrimination. However, failure to include any dates of employment is no solution to the problem. "If someone sends a résumé and they don't give any sense of how long they have been at a company, we assume the absolute worst," he says.

Another no-no, says the HR expert, is disguising a layoff or firing. "Don't send me a résumé that says, 'I've been working at a place from such-and-such a date to the present,' and then I find out you were laid off. Boom—right there you're dead in the water. . . . There might be a perfectly valid reason for a seemingly problematic issue, but you need to explain. If there is something negative, don't just expect HR managers to guess about it." If you were laid off—a fairly common event in a volatile job market—bring up the issue at the right time in the job-seeking process. Hiring experts say that while a layoff isn't the end of the world, there's no point in advertising it on your résumé. If and when you are called in for an interview and the topic arises, you can explain it at that point. Says one HR manager: "These days [being laid off] is less of a bad thing. Jobseekers can attribute it to downsizing or the phasing out of a function or position. It might be a question mark, but I don't think it will hurt [an applicant's prospects]."

Being fired, especially on account of performance, is obviously a harder burden to carry. Here, hiring experts advise leaving the word "firing" off your résumé, as it will send many employers scurrying. Instead, add your dates of employment and consider offering a brief explanation for your dismissal either in your cover letter or during an interview.

For more information on outwitting a firing, see chapter 7.

DON'T SAY "REFERENCES AVAILABLE UPON REQUEST"

It's common to include "References Available upon Request" or a similar tagline at the bottom of your résumé. In fact, it's almost as common as including your name at the top. But while your name is essential information, the "standby references" slogan doesn't serve any purpose. If a hiring manager invites you for an interview, he will expect you to furnish a list of professional references—period. By including a line about what is already expected of you, you will simply waste space. For more information on giving and preparing references, see chapter 6.

DON'T INCLUDE PERSONAL INFORMATION

When compiling their résumés, people sometimes feel compelled to add information that is not work-related. Sometimes they construct an "Other Information" section on their résumés that includes favorite hobbies, their pets' names, or how many children they have. While such tidbits are often a lot more interesting than work-related facts, it's not a good idea to include them. For one thing, these extra features take up valuable résumé space. And for another, many hiring managers view their inclusion as unprofessional.

It's probably a bad idea to include the fact that you love to ski, but it's definitely a bad idea to include your age, race, height, weight, marital status, or similar identifiers. Such personal information is just that—personal.

DO SEEK ASSISTANCE WITH YOUR RÉSUMÉ

Even if you're convinced that your résumé can't be improved upon, give it to a trusted friend for review. You might be surprised by the typos and grammatical errors she finds. A fresh pair of eyes is better than a pair that has been going over the same one or two pages for hours. In fact, the more eyes that critique your résumé, the better.

If you've never created a résumé before, don't hesitate to ask for outside help. If you're a student, take advantage of any "résumé-building" seminars your school might offer, or ask a trusted teacher or adviser to assist you. If you're not in school, do a little investigative work on the Internet or in the yellow pages. For a fee, an employment services company can help you to build a new résumé or to improve upon your existing version. Just be sure to ask about what you can expect and when you can expect it before you pay.

Whether or not you engage the help of others, it's a good idea to look at a variety of résumés to get a sense of alternate styles and formats. Ask to look at the résumés of other people in your desired industry, particularly those who have already found jobs. See which techniques work best, and don't hesitate to update your résumé accordingly. After all, as long as you are in the workforce, your résumé will always be a work-in-progress.

Example: "Before" Résumé

Alicia Jimenez

Alicia Jimenez
111 Any Avenue, Gainesville, FL 32611
Phone: (352) 000-0000   Fax: (352) 000-0000
Email: aliciajimenez@email.net

Experience

Features Writer/Editor, The Florida Log (student newspaper)

My job as the Features Writer/Editor of a student newspaper was
both fulfilling and challenging. Each week I wrote stories
on the student government. I also covered all political
activities on campus. Finally, I helped three freshmen student
reporters learn the ins and outs of running a student newspaper.

Summer Intern, The Daily Tribune

As a summer intern I helped to prepare news releases, manned the
phones, and did basic office work like faxing and copying. I also
helped to produce articles on local news pertaining to political
events.

Reporter, The Florida Log (student newspaper)

As a rookie reporter, I started at the low end of the totem pole.
Mostly I helped the editors with their stories and did any
administrative tasks they asked me to do.

Waitress, Margie's Café (high school job)

Working at Margie's Café, I waited on customers and made sure that
their food orders were satisfactory.

Skills

My computer skills include Microsoft Office, basic HTML, Adobe
Photoshop, and Adobe PageMaker. I am also good at performing
research using the Internet.

Courses I've taken include Advanced Newspaper Design, Advanced
Magazine Composition and Layout, and Intermediate Copywriting.

I am fluent in Spanish.

Awards/Activities

The Florida Press League named me as a merit scholarship
recipient. As for other activities, I am a member of the Society

of Environmental Journalists and a volunteer at the Student Crisis
Hotline Center.

Education

I have a BA from the University of Florida in Gainesville.   My
major was Journalism.   I graduated in May 2003 with a GPA of 3.4.

Hobbies

I enjoy hiking and fishing and most other outdoor activities.   I
also enjoy playing with my two dogs, Prince and Hero.

"BEFORE" RÉSUMÉ OF ALICIA JIMENEZ: COMMENTS

Alicia Jimenez's "Before" résumé needs some serious work. One of the most glaring problems is the formatting. While it's best to go easy on italics and bolt print, Jimenez decides to forgo any variations in her text. The result is that nothing stands out, not even the headings or her name.

While her résumé should follow reverse chronological order, the lack of dates makes it impossible to tell if it does. The lack of dates also precludes a hiring manager from knowing how long she worked at the *Florida Log* or the *Daily Tribune*. To gain credibility as a candidate, Jimenez must insert all dates of employment. She should also insert the location of the *Daily Tribune*. We can assume that her work at the *Florida Log* took place on campus.

As for her high school job as a waitress, this section should be deleted. Because Jimenez is a college graduate, there is a strong likelihood that at least four years have elapsed since she last worked at Margie's Café. The job is simply not relevant or timely enough to keep on her résumé. If Jimenez had worked at Margie's while attending college, however, she would probably want to keep this information. Employers are impressed by any candidate who can responsibly balance classes, extracurricular activities, and a job—even if the job is outside of the candidate's desired field.

Jimenez's descriptions could also use some improvement. She describes her tasks and skills using full sentences. Yet because a résumé calls for brevity, bulleted lists are a better option. Hiring managers would rather glance over important points than wade through whole paragraphs. Jimenez should also consider rephrasing her descriptions using action verbs. Instead of stating her accomplishments, she couches them in bland, passive language. For instance, she notes in the experience section: "I started at the low end of the totem pole. Mostly I helped the editors with their stories and did any administrative tasks they asked me to do." This description makes her sound meek—not an adjective that warms the hearts of hiring managers. Yet there's little question that the administrative tasks Jimenez performed were necessary to the day-to-day operations of the newspaper. Here is another way of describing her role, using more proactive and powerful language: "Provided special assistance to the editors, including researching story ideas, scheduling and performing interviews, and transcribing notes."

Because Jimenez graduated from college only a short time ago, she should bump the education section to the top of her résumé. She simply doesn't have enough work experience to merit listing her experience first. She should also provide an objective. Jimenez seeks a job in journalism—her summer internship, college newspaper experience, and major all point in that direction. Thus, there's no reason not to state her job preference. At the same time, she should word the objective in a general way. For example, if she wrote that she were interested in a position with the title of "Staff Reporter," she would limit her options. But if she wrote that she were looking for an "editorial position," she would open the door to more possibilities.

Finally, Jimenez should delete the hobbies section altogether. It's interesting that she enjoys outdoor activities and has two dogs, but this type of personal information does not enhance her employability. Besides, Jimenez needs to save space. For a recent graduate, her resume is too long.

Example: "After" Résumé

Alicia Jimenez

Alicia Jimenez
111 Any Avenue, Gainesville, FL 32611
Phone: (352) 000-0000   Fax: (352) 000-0000   E-mail: aliciajimenez@email.net

---

OBJECTIVE:

An editorial position with an established newspaper that would enable me to utilize my reporting skills and to contribute to a diverse and fast-paced work environment

EDUCATION:

University of Florida; Gainesville, Florida
BA, Journalism, Graduation: May 2003, GPA: 3.4

EXPERIENCE:

September 2002 - May 2003: Features Writer/Editor, the *Florida Log* (student newspaper)

- Reported on all political activities on campus, including rallies, meetings, and speeches
- Brainstormed, developed, and wrote weekly stories
- Supervised and mentored a team of three freshmen student reporters

June 2002 - August 2002: Summer Intern, the *Daily Tribune*, Gainesville, FL

- Assisted in the reporting, writing, and producing of articles on local news pertaining to political events
- Fact-checked news releases, including spot articles and feature articles
- Performed office duties such as document preparation and customer service assistance using a multi-line phone system

September 2001 - May 2002: Reporter, the *Florida Log* (student newspaper)

- Provided special assistance to the editors, including researching story ideas, scheduling and performing interviews, and transcribing notes

SKILLS:

Fluent in Spanish / MS Office / Basic HTML / Internet research / Adobe Photoshop, Adobe PageMaker, and QuarkXPress / Courses taken include Advanced Newspaper Design, Advanced Magazine Composition and Layout, and Intermediate Copywriting

AWARDS/ACTIVITIES:

- Merit scholarship recipient, the Florida Press League, 2001
- Current member, Society of Environmental Journalists
- Volunteer, Student Crisis Hotline Center, September 2000 - May 2003

Example: "Before" Résumé

Jonathan Hope

RÉSUMÉ

Jonathan Hope
25 Random Road North #1234
Atlanta, GA 30320
Phone: (404) 000-0000
E-mail: jhope@anyemail.com

ABOUT ME: Experienced and highly motivated marketing professional with
a proven track record in direct marketing, strategic planning,
promotions, and marketing communications

MY EXPERIENCE:

July 1998 – Dec. 1999	**The Rivertin Association, Chicago, IL** *Marketing Advisor*

                                   - Developed short- and long-range marketing plans,
budgets, and online and offline
marketing programs for a sports facility
- Conducted market and customer research to
identify knew trends that have the potential
to impact service offerings
- Wrote, edited, and prodused a monthly marketing
newsletter for the company

Jan. 2000 – March 2002	**Barnard Marketing Services, Atlanta, GA** *Marketing Consultant*

- Partnered with clients to identify opportunities
across their businesses and made recommendations
where appropriate
- Created and implemented direct and email
marketing strategies and best practices for supply
chain management solutions provider and its
business units
- Reviewed and recommended changes to current
systems
- Developed collateral materials, Web sites, and
public relations vehicles
- Reason for leaving the company: I outgrew my
position

May 2002 – Present	**FLR Corporation, Atlanta, GA** *Associate Marketing Director*

- Developed cost-cutting marketing strategies
- Led teem in delivering strategic direct
marketing programs

```
                            - Managed the teem's financials
                            - Reason for leaving the company: I was fired

    MY EDUCATION:

    1992 - 1996        Attended the University of Tennessee, Knoxville, TN
                       Bachelor of Science degree in Economics with a miner in
                       Political Science.  3.8 GPA.

    1996 - 1998        Attended the Terry College of Business, Athens, GA
                       Master of Business Administration degree.  3.6 GPA.


    MY REFERENCES:

    Abigail Hutchinson
    14 Hillcrest Street
    Staten Island, NY 10304

    Lan Shen
    44 State Street, Apt. 321
    Atlanta, GA 30320

    Aquitha Winterson
    30 Gunther Drive
    Chicago, IL 60619
```

"BEFORE" RÉSUMÉ OF JONATHAN HOPE: COMMENTS

The "Before" résumé of Jonathan Hope could use some sprucing up. Hope labels all parts of his résumé, but doesn't do so correctly. He doesn't need to write the word "résumé" across the top, for instance. Nor does he need to use the personal possessive pronoun "my" to preface the other headings like "Experience" and "Education." To Hope's credit, the headings are in the correct order. Unfortunately, the sequence of entries under the headings are not. They should be in reverse chronological order.

Hope has a number of misspellings in his résumé. He writes "knew" instead of "new," "prodused" instead of "produced," "teem" instead of "team," and "miner" instead of "minor." Note that most spell checker programs would not pick up errors like "knew," "teem," and "miner" since these are real words, but used in the wrong context. Therefore, Hope should definitely ask a knowledgeable friend to double-check his résumé for errors.

Most hiring managers would find Hope's descriptions inadequate. He doesn't offer enough detail, nor does he quantify his results. For example, in a description for his job at The Rivertin Association, Hope writes, "Developed short- and long-range marketing plans, budgets, and online and offline marketing programs for a sports facility." Hiring managers, though, would be more interested in knowing how Hope's work paid off fiscally. They would prefer a description that offers numbers, such as, "Developed short- and long-range marketing plans, budgets, and online and offline marketing programs for a sorts facility with average annual sales of U.S. $51,000,000. Increased inquires by 25 percent and sales by 15 percent from January 1998 to May 1999."

A potentially disastrous aspect of Hope's résumé is his explanation of why he left two former employers. It is unnecessary for Hope to cite why he left these companies. But even if it were necessary, by writing that he "was fired" from FLR Corporation, Hope virtually demolishes his chances of getting an interview. If Hope feels it is absolutely necessary to mention the firing and to offer an explanation for it, he should do so in a cover letter—not in his résumé.

Under the education heading, Hope says he "attended" both the University of Tennessee and the Terry College of Business. To employers, a red flag goes up whenever candidates mention they "attended" school because it means they might not have graduated. If Hope did in fact graduate from the schools he lists, he should say so explicitly.

Hope writes in his Personal Career Inventory that he received two awards: the United States Marketing Association's Excellence Award for Creative Vision, and the Georgia Marketing Association's Crystal Award. Because both of these awards are in Hope's chosen field, marketing, its puzzling that he doesn't include them in his résumé. He should definitely do so. What he shouldn't include, though, are his references. Hope should give his references at a later stage in the hiring process, once he is invited for an interview. At that point, he should list his references on a separate sheet of paper and he should make sure that he incudes all the relevant information, including job titles, company names, daytime phone numbers, and e-mail addresses.

Example: "After" Résumé

Jonathan Hope

JONATHAN HOPE
25 Random Road North #1234, Atlanta, GA 30320
Phone: (404) 000-0000 E-mail: jhope@anyemail.com

SUMMARY OF QUALIFICATIONS: Experienced and highly motivated marketing professional with a proven track record in direct marketing, strategic planning, promotions, and marketing communications

BUSINESS EXPERIENCE:

May 2002 -   **FLR Corporation, Atlanta, GA**
Present   *Associate Marketing Director*

- Developed cost-cutting marketing strategies that led to a savings of over U.S. $300,000 from May to December 2002
- Led team in delivering strategic direct marketing programs across offline and online channels
- Managed the team's financials, meeting contribution margin goals

Jan. 2000 -   **Barnard Marketing Services, Atlanta, GA**
March 2002   *Marketing Consultant*

- Partnered with clients to identify opportunities across their businesses and made recommendations where appropriate
- Created and implemented direct and email marketing strategies and best practices for supply chain management solutions provider and its business units
- Reviewed and recommended changes to current systems to more effectively leverage marketing opportunities. Assisted staff with implementation of initial changes
- Developed collateral materials, web sites, and public relations vehicles for clients ranging from professional services firms to retailers

July 1998 -   **The Rivertin Association, Chicago, IL**
Dec. 1999   *Marketing Advisor*

- Developed short- and long-range marketing plans, budgets, and online and offline marketing programs for a sports facility with average annual sales of U.S. $51,000.000. Increased inquiries 25 percent and sales by 15 percent from January 1998 to May 1999
- Conducted market and customer research to identify new trends that have the potential to impact service offerings. Integrated findings into strategic planning and shared the results with all department heads via an online presentation
- Wrote, edited, and produced a monthly marketing newsletter for the company

EDUCATION:

1996 - 1998   The Terry College of Business, Athens, GA
              Master of Business Administration degree. Graduation: May 1998. 3.6 GPA

1992 - 1996   The University of Tennessee, Knoxville, TN
              Bachelor of Science degree in Economics with a minor in Political Science. Graduation: May 1996. 3.8 GPA.

HONORS AND AWARDS:

2002 Recipient, United States Marketing Association's Excellence Award for Creative Vision
2001 Recipient, Georgia Marketing Association's Crystal Award

Key Chapter Points

✦ The best résumé is not one that includes every last detail of your work experience, but one that get noticed by hiring managers. Everything about your résumé, from format, to font, to language, should be tailored toward that end.

✦ It is essential to customize your résumé to suit each job for which you are applying. In customizing your résumé, look not only at information in the job advertisement, but also at the notes you've collected in your Prospective Employer List and, if applicable, on an informational interview.

✦ Use dynamic and vivid language in your résumé, especially action verbs that connote authority and competence.

✦ Format your résumé in a way that will enable companies to scan it electronically. Scanning is a common practice among many employers. It allows hiring managers to search through all the résumés they've received for specific information and keywords.

✦ Seek assistance when building a new résumé or when editing an existing version. The more eyes that see your résumé, the better your chances of avoiding typos, spelling and grammatical errors, and other résumé blunders.

Chapter Five

CONQUERING THE COVER LETTER

Few one-page documents have inspired more angst and chewed-up pencils than the cover letter. This chapter will tell you what you need to know to turn what appears to be an arduous project into something that is quite doable.

Like any great pairing, the résumé and cover letter work in tandem. Think Laurel and Hardy without the humor. Think Bonnie and Clyde without the crime spree. Think peanut butter and jelly without the stickiness. While the résumé provides a clear-cut rundown of your employment qualifications, the cover letter is more like a sidekick. It offers the reader a few choice pieces of information, all of which should correspond with the skills and experience required for the job. The cover letter should also offer a glimpse of your "softer" professional qualifications: your ability to communicate, your attention to detail, and your personal understanding of why you would be a worthwhile addition to the company. While not every job listing specifically requests a cover letter, it's always of benefit to include one. In fact, even if you're applying for a position that isn't being publicly advertised, send a cover letter. Along with your résumé, the cover letter provides the information necessary for an employer to decide whether to bring you in for an interview.

Like the résumé, the cover letter must be tailored to each specific company. Hiring managers can tell right away when someone has taken the time to research a company and to revise his cover letter accordingly, as opposed to someone who sends out the same tired cover letter again and again. As with your résumé, your Prospective Employer List will be useful as you tweak your cover letter to reflect the unique attributes of each company.

The cover letter's purpose is not simply to rehash bits and pieces of your résumé. Rather, the cover letter should address the questions that are of interest to any hiring manager. Why do you want the job? Why are you qualified for the job? Why do you want to work for this company as opposed to any other? Here, of course, having a real understanding of what makes a company tick will enable you to answer these questions with greater ease. Says one HR employee at a strategy consulting firm: "I'm always impressed when a cover letter is meaningful, when the person knows a thing or two about the company beyond the information that is up on our Website."

In terms of format and style, the cover letter should be formal, but not unduly formal. Use a professional tone that is conversational rather than cold or colorful. Use high-grade paper—but make sure it's light-colored. Like the résumé, your cover letter may be scanned into an electronic database. Dark-colored paper or any ink other than black can impede the scanning process. Use one standard font, use it throughout the page, and be sure to include any keywords and catch phrases that are relevant to your industry or career area.

Your cover letter should be composed of paragraphs, although the occasional set of bulleted points can work—used sparingly. Most importantly, your cover letter should flawlessly relay your information. Beth Camp, the owner of a placement service, says, "A good cover letter is expected. A bad cover letter will sink you before you start."

Anatomy of a Cover Letter

FORMAT

DATE

The date should appear at the top of page, but the justification—left, middle, or right—is entirely up to you. It's better to write out the month rather than to use an all-numbers format—July 7, 2003 as opposed to 7/7/03.

YOUR NAME AND ADDRESS

Your name and address come below the date. These items should correspond with the contact information listed on your résumé. Don't use an address or name spelling that is different from what is on your résumé, as such an inconsistency will confuse hiring managers. You can include your phone number and e-mail address here too, unless you wish to add them to the last paragraph of your cover letter (see "Third Paragraph").

NOTE: If you're using your own personal letterhead, there is no need to repeat your name and address again.

THE NAME, TITLE, AND ADDRESS OF THE RECIPIENT

In many cases, the name, title, and address of the person to whom you're sending your cover letter will appear right in the job ad. This is the best-case scenario, as you don't have to do any additional work. If you already have all the information you need, add it directly below your own contact information in the following order: person's full name, person's title, company name, and company address.

If you don't have one or more parts of this information, put on your Sherlock Holmes hat and prepare to do a little investigating. You can always find out a company's address via the phone book or by doing an Internet search. However, tracking down a contact's name and title may be more difficult. One alternative is to call the company directly and to ask to be put through to human resources. Once you reach someone from that department, explain that you are assembling a cover letter for such-and-such a position—if there is a job number, it helps to have it on hand—and that you want the recipient's name so that you can address the letter properly. The human resources representative may or may not give you the information you need. If he does, great. If not, you can always resort to a more general greeting such as one of the examples listed below.

GREETING

The greeting used almost universally in cover letters is "Dear," followed by a courtesy title like "Mr." or "Ms.," followed by the person's last name. You'll want to avoid using "Miss" or "Mrs." when addressing a woman, as these titles indicate marital status, something that you have no way of knowing and that is not, in any case, workplace relevant. Examples of this standard cover letter salutation include "Dear Mr. Truong" or "Dear Ms. Hadamitzky." If the contact's first name is unusual or gender neutral—Regan or Cory or Lee, for example—you can simply write "Dear," followed by the person's first name, followed by the person's last name. Examples include "Dear Hillary O'Brian" or "Dear Radha Singh." Use a colon {:} rather than a comma {,} after the greeting, as the colon indicates formality while the comma is more casual.

If you don't know the person's name and are unable to find out what it is, try a general standby such as "Dear Hiring Manager." Two old-fashioned variations are "Dear Sir or Madam" or "To Whom It May Concern." Both are acceptable in lieu of the person's actual name.

THE BODY OF THE COVER LETTER

The body of your cover letter should consist of three—or if absolutely necessary, four—paragraphs. While you want to provide all the relevant points, you don't want to inundate the reader with too much information. A cover letter that exceeds four paragraphs or one page is simply too long.

The most common cover letter is three paragraphs long, with each paragraph serving a distinct purpose. Below is an overview of what each paragraph should contain.

FIRST PARAGRAPH

The first paragraph serves as a brief introduction to who you are and what job you are applying for. Often, the first sentence tells the reader which position you want, including the job number, if listed. The second sentence usually gives the reader a general sense of your qualifications. If you're a recent college graduate, for example, the first paragraph might start like this: "Please consider me for a Sales Representative IV position (Job Number 0087800) with Dell Computer Corporation. A recent graduate of the University of Southern California, with a degree in Business Administration, I believe my education and previous sales experience as a summer intern with eMachines Inc. would enable me to make a first-rate contribution to your company."

If you've been referred to the position by another person, such as someone who works within the company, be sure to include this information in the first paragraph. Because referrals account for so many hirings, it's essential that you mention your referrer's name early in the letter in order to attract the reader's interest. Here is one example of how you might introduce your referrer: "Joline Finch, a Software Configuration Manager at your headquarters in Austin, suggested that I send my application materials to your attention."

If you wish, you can also include where you saw the advertised position (on Monster or HotJobs, in a newspaper, on the company's Website, etc.). All in all, the first paragraph should emphasize your status as a promising applicant and leave the reader wanting to learn more about you.

SECOND PARAGRAPH

The second paragraph is your best opportunity to shine in the cover letter. Here, you can further elaborate on why you're qualified for the position. You have plenty of flexibility in the second paragraph. However, you have to remember that you are trying to impress companies with what you can offer them, not necessarily what they can offer you. It would be unwise to speak at length about what you would gain by joining the company.

Take the cues offered in the job advertisement to speak about how your skills or previous employment experience can help accommodate each employer's individual needs. Be concrete and specific in your explanations. Cite accomplishments from the past that are relevant to the position for which you are applying. For example, if you have previous experience in business development, you might say, "My four years of experience in business development with the Gallup Organization would enable me to make a meaningful contribution to your corporation, especially in the field of education, where I have proven my ability to introduce senior executives at higher-level institutions to new client solutions." If your experience doesn't directly address a company's needs, don't worry. You can always put a spin on your information so that the most relevant aspects are apparent. Say, for instance, you are a college graduate with no work experience and that you are interested in working at a nonprofit organization such as the World Wildlife Federation. You might speak of how your ability to organize a volunteer committee to clean up a park, for instance, shows your leadership skills, and how those skills would be transferable to a position at the organization.

No matter what your level of experience, avoid broad, overarching statements that aren't backed up by solid facts. Steer clear of writing sweeping declarations like, "Obviously, I would be great addition to your team," or "I'm smart, experienced, and can do the job as well as anybody," or "I'm good at multitasking and would be happy to multitask in this position." Such statements will only do more harm than good, as hiring managers will notice that you haven't made much effort to communicate effectively or to customize your cover letter.

Include in the second paragraph, too, a display of your knowledge of the company. From your information-gathering for your Prospective Employer List, you should be aware of recent news and goings-on at each employer, including mergers, acquisitions, new product launches, etc. Hiring managers will be impressed if you can incorporate this information into your cover letter and, at the same time, address how you would be able to contribute to the bottom line. For example, say you have consumer product marketing experience and that you are interested in getting a position at Frito-Lay, the snack foods company. Say you know from company press releases that Frito-Lay is introducing a new line of potato chips. Here, you might speak of one or two of your marketing achievements, then add how your experience might be of use in launching the company's new product. Voilà—you will have succeeded in showing both resourcefulness and an awareness of the company's current needs.

OPTIONAL MIDDLE PARAGRAPH

As mentioned earlier, most cover letters are no more than three paragraphs. However, if you feel compelled to add additional information about how your work experience, accomplishments, and education are relevant to the job, you can do so here. You can also use this paragraph, rather than the second, to display a knowledge of the employer.

Other people use the optional middle paragraph to explain inconsistencies in their résumés. This is your opportunity to anticipate any questions that a hiring manager might have. If you are a parent, for example, and took several years off to raise your children, you can state that information here so that hiring managers understand why there is a gap in your work history. Perhaps you didn't finish your graduate degree program, and thus didn't put a date of graduation on your résumé. Here is a place to explain why, without going into too much detail. Perhaps you decided to relocate, or perhaps you decided that reentering the workforce would be more rewarding than continuing your program.

What the optional third paragraph is not is a place to spill your guts. You should resist the urge to write in an overtly personal way. If part of the reason you left school early is because you despised your academic adviser, for instance, keep that information to yourself. Remember that the cover letter is essentially a formal document and that your readers are not looking for an emotional outpouring. No matter what your circumstances, keep your tone positive and professional.

THIRD PARAGRAPH

The third, or final paragraph is your chance to wrap up the cover letter and to express your interest in hearing back from the employer. Here, you'll want to mention that your résumé has been enclosed, if you are sending your documents by regular mail, or attached, if you are sending your documents by e-mail. Alternatively, you can add a single line at the bottom of your cover letter, below your closing, such as "Enclosed: résumé" or "Please see attached résumé."

Don't forget to include your phone number and e-mail address too, if you haven't already mentioned this information at the top of the page. If you've been asked to include salary requirements, you can do so here (see "Common Cover Letter Mistakes," below). You might also want to write a last enthusiastic remark about the company or the position.

The best way to close the cover letter is with a thank you, followed by a polite request for a response from the employer. One common cover letter ending is, "Thank you for your time. I hope to hear from you at your earliest convenience." Another goes like this: "I appreciate your consideration and I look forward to hearing from you." Some professionals take the initiative and add a sentence about following up such as, "I'll call your office on Wednesday of next week to see if you would like to discuss the possibility of my contributing to your company." This is a smart, proactive way to indicate your sincere interest in the job, and perhaps, to have meaningful contact with someone in a position to hire you.

However you decide to sum up your letter, stay polite and don't go overboard. It is the unwise jobseeker who ends her note by saying effusively, "I can't wait to be interviewed for this position, which I'm perfect for. I look forward to hearing from you by the end of the day!"

CLOSING

To end your cover letter, be sure to use a professional closing like "Sincerely," or "Best," or "Best Regards," or "Kind Regards," or "Respectfully Yours." If you are sending your cover letter by regular mail, add your signature at the bottom, then type out your name below it. If you are sending your cover letter by e-mail, however, you can simply use your typewritten name.

Common Cover Letter Mistakes

MISSPELLING WORDS AND USING POOR GRAMMAR

Hiring managers have a low threshold for mistakes in spelling and grammar. They figure that if this candidate hasn't made the effort to edit his own cover letter, he probably isn't going to be a conscientious and detail-oriented employee.

Hiring managers are even more appalled when the spelling error occurs in their own names. Therefore, check name spellings twice and make sure you're not confusing "Johnston" for "Johnson," for instance. The same advice that is true of résumés (chapter 4) is true for cover letters—use the spell-check feature and have at least one knowledgeable friend do a thorough read-through.

USING INCORRECT OR MISSING TITLES

If the name and title of the cover letter recipient is not posted in the job ad, and a thorough attempt to find out the person's information has met with failure, it's acceptable to address your letter to the "hiring manager" or to use another generic greeting. If, however, the name and title of the person have been posted in the job ad, and you've failed to include it, the recipient won't be pleased. Says one Chicago-based recruiter: "That's a strike, definitely. I mean, how would you feel if you received a piece of mail addressed to 'Dear Anonymous'?" According to this recruiter, it's also a strike to use the wrong title when you address the cover letter recipient. A recipient may feel especially annoyed or slighted if you use a title that doesn't reflect his seniority—"Assistant Director" rather than "Director," for example.

OVERDOING THE CREATIVITY

"I know people who have sent videos instead of cover letters—that backfires. Don't do it," says Beth Camp, a recruiter. She says that cover letters are the "expected protocol"; jobseekers shouldn't veer too far from the norm. "Some people add their pictures, especially in e-mails. Again, don't do it," Camp warns. "It never comes out looking very good, and [hiring personnel] will laugh it off." Camp says to rely on common sense when deciding what to incorporate into a cover letter and what to leave out. "Don't do anything too unusual if you're going into a company that is very staid and very conservative," she explains. "But if you're submitting a cover letter to MTV, you can be a little bit more creative than if you're submitting a cover letter to Goldman Sachs."

SOUNDING TOO BOASTFUL OR TOO MEEK

The cover letter is the place to tout one's skills and accomplishments, especially as they relate to the job posting. However, candidates stand a definite danger of seeming egotistical if they pat themselves on the back too much. "There's a fine line between being confident and being conceited," says the Chicago-based recruiter. "You don't want to straddle that line. You want to land squarely on the side of confident." How can you avoid making this mistake? Speak of what you have to offer exclusively in the context of what the employer needs. That way, you'll stand less of a chance of rambling off a list of accomplishments that have little bearing on what you'd be doing on the job. Also, avoid grandiose statements that you can't possibly back up, such as "I'm the best salesman in the Midwest" or "My track record for satisfying clients is second to none."

By the same token, you don't want to sound humble or meek. The best way to portray yourself in a cover letter is to present accomplishments that relate to the job, then buttress them with solid evidence. Rather than saying, "I'm the ultimate customer service representative," for example, you might say, "At my previous employer, Abbott's Electronics, I responded to a minimum of forty customer service calls daily. I'm proud to say that my strong understanding of customer relationship management principles enabled me to resolve issues quickly and to the satisfaction of both parties. In fact, over the last ten months an average of only 7 percent of customers needed to call for repeat assistance."

USING HUMOR

As with the résumé, the cover letter should not contain humor, sarcasm, or anything above or beyond the boundaries of professionalism. Even if you're known for your clever witticisms, keep them to yourself. Outwitting the job market will require patience, intelligence, and unwavering persistence, but it won't (unfortunately!) require a good joke.

Be wary, too, of an unduly familiar tone. How you would write to a good buddy is not how you would write to the hiring manager at the company of your dreams.

COPYING YOUR RÉSUMÉ

Remember, your cover letter and résumé are partners. They should complement each other, but they should not mimic one another word for word. A common cover letter mistake is to repeat text from your résumé without adding anything new. It's okay on a cover letter to cite an accomplishment that you've also posted on your résumé, but you must offer a twist. Go into further detail, or explain how this accomplishment marked a watershed in your career. You don't want to bore your reader, so if you choose to recycle information, be sure to do so in a new and enlightening way.

INCLUDING YOUR SALARY REQUIREMENTS

Some job ads require applicants to include their salary requirements. In such instances, you have little choice but to include a salary that would be acceptable given your work experience, location, and previous earnings. If you must mention a salary, mention a range—that is, what your lowest acceptable salary would be through to a moderate sum. Examples include "in the range of $40,000" or from $35,000 to $45,000." You can also say, "$40,000-negotiable."

If a job ad does not explicitly ask for salary requirements, it's best to exclude them. The chances are great that you'll ask for an amount too low or too high, as you may have no basis for knowing what individual employers are willing to pay. Besides, the best time to talk salary is after you've been offered a job—not before you've come in for an interview.

SOUNDING LIKE EVERYONE ELSE

While you don't want to tip the scales of creativity, you don't want to sound boring either. Think about what sets you apart. Think about the ways in which you are different from other candidates applying for the job. Once you have determined what makes you a unique candidate, address the issue in your cover letter—but make sure you keep the requirements of the job in mind. Busy hiring managers sometimes review a cover letter only if a candidate's résumé is promising. Make sure their time is well spent with a cover letter that entices.

Example: "Before" Cover Letter

Alicia Jimenez
111 Any Avenue
Gainesville, FL 32611

The Florida Daily News
Attention: Mrs. Sophia Cuomo, Hiring Manager
120 Anonymous Drive, Suite 304
Orlando, FL 32801

Dear Mrs. Cuomo:

I noticed the open position of Staff Writer (Job Number 30874) with The Florida Daily News and I want the job.

As the former Features Writer/Editor of The Florida Log, a student newspaper, I reported on all political activities on campus, including rallies, meetings, and speeches. During my 2002 summer internship with The Daily Tribune in Gainesville, Florida, I fact-checked news releases, including spot articles and features articles. I also performed office duties such as document preparation and customer service assistance using a multi-line phone system.

I'm a hard worker and I know I would be the perfect person for the position. In this envelope I've included a copy of my résumé and three clips. If you have any questions, you can contact me by phone at (352) 000-0000 or by e-mail at gainesvillegirl@coolchick.com.

See You Soon,

(SIGNATURE)

Alicia Jimenez

"BEFORE" COVER LETTER OF ALICIA JIMENEZ: COMMENTS

Alicia Jimenez wouldn't impress many people with her "Before" cover letter. She makes far too many mistakes. Fortunately, these mistakes can be easily remedied with a little editing.

For the most part, the formatting of the cover letter is good, although Jimenez forgets to add a date at the top. Another gaffe is that she uses the title "Mrs." when addressing Sophia Cuomo, the hiring manager. Even if Sophia Cuomo were married, Jimenez should stick to the neutral title of "Ms." when addressing female professionals. Jimenez makes a more subtle mistake when writing the *Florida Daily News,* the *Florida Log,* and the *Daily Tribune.* The names of periodicals should always be italicized or underlined. This error might go unnoticed if she weren't applying for a job at a newspaper, where a knowledge of proper punctuation and typography is essential.

While Jimenez does remember to use no more than three or four paragraphs in the body of her cover letter, she could do a much better job of presenting her information. In the first paragraph, she writes, "I noticed the open position of Staff Writer (Job Number 30874) with *The Florida Daily News* and I want the job." Here, Jimenez forgets to introduce her credentials and qualifications. But more importantly, she makes the mistake of stating what she wants instead of what she can offer. Many employers will be put off by her self-serving tone.

In the second paragraph, Jimenez doesn't tailor her cover letter to the individual job opening. Instead, she repeats parts of her résumé word for word. Jimenez also forgets a chance to show the newspaper that she's done her research. She makes no reference to any shifts or changes the company is currently experiencing.

Jimenez seriously botches the first sentence of the third paragraph when she writes, "I'm a hard worker and I know I would be the perfect person for the position." Nowhere in her cover letter does Jimenez support this bold declaration with facts about her performance or the results

Example: "After" Cover Letter

June 3, 20XX

Alicia Jimenez
111 Any Avenue
Gainesville, FL 32611

The *Florida Daily News*
Attention: Sophia Cuomo, Hiring Manager
120 Anonymous Drive, Suite 304
Orlando, FL 32801

Dear Ms. Cuomo:

Please consider me for the position of Staff Writer (Job Number 30874) with the *Florida Daily News*. A recent graduate of the University of Florida with a BA in Journalism, I believe my education and previous reporting experience make me a strong contender for the job.

According to the job description, your paper is looking for a self-starter who can assist the editorial staff with the quick turnaround of stories. I am pleased to say that as the Features Writer/Editor of the *Florida Log*, a student newspaper, I proved my ability to produce clean, crisp copy in an expeditious manner. My 2002 summer internship with the *Daily Tribune* in Gainesville, Florida gave me exposure to and experience in the operations of a daily paper. During this internship I consistently met my deadlines and worked closely with the editorial team researching story ideas, primarily on local political issues. I believe this experience would be highly relevant to the job of Staff Writer since your paper recently expanded its political coverage.

I am very excited about the position of Staff Writer and would welcome the opportunity to meet with you to discuss how I could contribute to the team. As requested, I've enclosed a copy of my résumé and three clips. If you have any questions, please feel free to contact me by phone at (352) 000-0000 or by e-mail at aliciajimenez@email.net.

Kind Regards,

(SIGNATURE)

Alicia Jimenez

she's capable of achieving. Thus, the statement becomes meaningless, if not damaging. Jimenez also errs when she gives a different e-mail address (gainesvillegirl@coolchick.com) from the one she lists in her résumé (aliciajimenez@email.net). To simplify communication with the hiring manager, Jimenez should make sure her e-mail is exactly the same on all her documents. This one e-mail address, moreover, should sound professional—something that gainesvillegirl@coolchick.com does not.

The last snafu in the cover letter is the closing. Instead of a courteous closing like "Sincerely" or "Best Regards," Jimenez opts for the colloquial and unsuitable "See You Soon." But if the hiring manager were to read this "Before" cover letter, she would probably hope to see Jimenez later rather than sooner.

"BEFORE" COVER LETTER OF JONATHAN HOPE: COMMENTS

Jonathan Hope doesn't have a hope in the world with this "Before" cover letter. At first glance, the cover letter seems strong. Hope remembers to include the date, his own address, and the name and address of the company. But he quickly stumbles when greeting the hiring manager. He uses a different version of the hiring manager's name (Mr. Arten) from the one he writes earlier (Alton T. Arden).

The first paragraph of the cover letter is quite good. Hope does everything he is supposed to do, including expressing interest in the position, naming the employee at Magic Fountain Multimedia who referred him, and briefly outlining his professional qualifications. Yet the second paragraph ruins any positive momentum inspired by the first. Hope makes two grandiose remarks: "I think everyone on the team would agree that it was my superb leadership that paved the path toward success" and "There is no question that the company would have suffered financial setbacks if it weren't for my fine performance." Hope probably wished to impress the hiring manager with these statements. Instead, he shows himself to be egotistical. Companies are looking for

Example: "Before" Cover Letter

September 3, 20XX

Jonathan Hope
25 Random Road North #1234
Atlanta, GA 30320

Alton T. Arden
Human Resources Manager
Magic Fountain Multimedia
41 Apple Street, Suite 100
Brooklyn, NY 11231

Dear Mr. Arten:

I write to express strong interest in the Director of Marketing position. Alexandra Hong, a manager in your Business Development department, suggested I contact you. As the current Associate Marketing Director of FLR Corporation in Atlanta, I have over five years of professional marketing experience, a track record of excellence, and a Master of Business Administration from The Terry College of Business. I believe my education and business experience would enable me to make a valuable contribution to your company.

Under my management, the marketing team at FLR Corporation successfully delivered strategic direct marketing programs across offline and online channels. I think everyone on the team would agree that it was my superb leadership that paved the path toward success. As the Associate Marketing Director at FLR, I also managed the team's financials and consistently met contribution margin goals. There is no question that the company would have suffered financial setbacks if it weren't for my fine performance.

My high level of motivation has been recognized by all of my previous employers and I have risen quickly to positions of greater responsibility throughout my career. In addition, I have demonstrated an ability to assemble, mentor, and retain dynamic marketing teams.

Please keep in mind that I'm looking for a salary of at least U.S. $85,000. If you're interested in learning more about me, you can contact me at (404) 000-0000 or by e-mail at jhope@anyemail.com.

Sincerely,
Jonathan Hope

leaders, but they are also looking for team players—something that Hope doesn't appear to be. He should have foregone the pretentious remarks, and instead highlighted his achievements with quantifiable results.

In the optional middle paragraph, Hope points out some of his accomplishments, but he could have gone further and introduced information that shows he is familiar with Magic Fountain Multimedia, and specifically, its marketing efforts. Additionally, in either this paragraph or the second paragraph, he should have added more industry-specific catch phrases and client names. Once Hope sends his cover letter and résumé, there is a good chance both documents will be scanned into an online database, which will then be searched for key words.

In the final paragraph, Hope decides to assert his salary requirements. This is a bold move and an unwise one. Any discussion of compensation should occur later in the hiring process, preferably after the company has extended an offer. Hope should, however, make mention of his résumé. Unfortunately, he forgets to say whether he has included it. Hope also misses a great opportunity when he decides to take a passive approach toward further contact. Hope could have mentioned that he will follow up with a phone call or e-mail. Instead, he asks the hiring manager to contact him.

Hope's final mistake is leaving no room for his signature at the bottom of the page. If Hope decides to e-mail his cover letter, a signature is unnecessary. However, if he decides to send it via fax or regular mail, he should definitely sign his name above the typewritten version.

Example: "After" Cover Letter

September 3, 20XX

Jonathan Hope
25 Random Road North #1234
Atlanta, GA 30320

Alton T. Arden
Human Resources Manager
Magic Fountain Multimedia
41 Apple Street, Suite 100
Brooklyn, NY 11231

Dear Mr. Arden:

I write to express strong interest in the Director of Marketing position at your company. Alexandra Hong, a manager in your Business Development department, suggested I contact you. As the current Associate Marketing Director of FLR Corporation in Atlanta, I have over five years of professional marketing experience, a track record of excellence, and a Master of Business Administration from the Terry College of Business. Below, I've cited some of my achievements that show my ability to deliver results:

- Led team at FLR in delivering strategic direct marketing programs across offline and online channels that resulted in a 50 percent increase in sales from May to December 2002

- Provided the vision and managed the implementation of a U.S. $5,000,000 marketing campaign for a major consumer products company that led to a 25 percent increase in revenue from March to November 2001

- Developed innovative marketing strategies for clients such as The Clorox Company, General Mills, Procter & Gamble, Unilever, and Colgate-Palmolive

My high level of motivation has been recognized by all of my previous employers, and I have risen quickly to positions of greater responsibility throughout my career. In addition, I have demonstrated an ability to assemble, mentor, and retain dynamic marketing teams. I'm confident that I can achieve similar success at Magic Fountain Multimedia, especially in the area of online marketing, a sector I understand you are expanding.

I would very much appreciate the opportunity to meet with you to learn more about Magic Fountain Multimedia and the position of Director of Marketing. Enclosed is my résumé for your review. I will be in New York City early next week and I will contact you then to inquire about the status of your search. In the meantime, please contact me at (404) 000-0000 or by e-mail at jhope@anyemail.com if you need additional information.

Sincerely,

(SIGNATURE)

Jonathan Hope

Key Chapter Points

✦ Always send a cover letter when you send a résumé. While a good cover letter is expected, a poorly written one can ruin your chances of moving along in the hiring process.

✦ The résumé and cover letter work in tandem. Each should complement the other, but information that is mentioned in the résumé should be repeated in the cover letter only in a way that sheds new light on your qualifications and that is uniquely pertinent to each employer's needs.

✦ The body of any cover letter is comprised of three or, at the most, four paragraphs, each of which serves a distinct purpose. While the basic rules of cover letter construction must be obeyed, you can set yourself apart by identifying your unique professional attributes and illustrating them in concrete and specific ways.

✦ Among the most common of cover letter mistakes is using incorrect or missing titles, sounding too boastful or too meek, and including your salary requirements when they have not been requested.

Chapter Six

THE APPLICATION PROCESS

Whew—you're almost there. You've assessed what you have to offer an employer and what you want out of one. You've researched many companies and whittled down your list to an elite few. You've learned how, when, and why to network. You've fine-tuned your résumé and cover letter so that they are the envy of every jobseeker in town.

Now's the time to showcase all the work you've done. The grand finale is at hand—it's time to send out your résumé and cover letter.

How you apply to a job advertisement is nearly as important as what you put in your résumé and cover letter. You have to make sure not only that you are addressing your application materials to the right person, but also that you are sending them in the way that is most convenient for that person. Finally, you have to make sure that you haven't made any errors along the way.

Methods of Applying for a Job

To start, find out how the recipient wants to receive your résumé and cover letter. If you're applying to a job that you've seen posted in a newspaper or online job board, the submission information should be right there. Most of the time there is a name and physical address for regular mailings, or an e-mail address for online mailings. If for some reason no submission information is posted, call the company and speak with a representative in the human resources department. Ask for the name and title of the hiring manager responsible for the position, and how that person would prefer you apply. Don't forget to verify the spelling of the person's name.

Your Prospective Employer List is an extremely useful tool for keeping track of the jobs you are applying for. In the "Notes" section, keep a running tally of the positions you applied for (and job numbers, if included) at each company, the dates you applied, the methods in which you applied, and the names and titles of the hiring managers to whom you've addressed your materials. As you move along in the hiring process, you'll also want to include the dates you followed up, and a detailed record of any correspondence you've had with each company. You should also keep copies of each tailored cover letter and résumé you send out—even if you're simply saving them onto the hard drive of your computer. If you are invited for an interview, you'll want to know exactly what information you've already given an employer.

APPLYING FOR JOBS VIA REGULAR MAIL

Though the majority of companies now prefer applicants to apply for jobs online (or, in rare cases, via fax), a minority prefer to receive résumés and cover letters via regular mail. This is, in most cases, the most straightforward way to apply for a job. Simply enclose your résumé and cover letter in a large envelope. (Don't fold your materials into a letter-size envelope, as papers with creases can't be scanned as easily.) Be sure the envelope is addressed to the right person in the right department—and that you have sufficient postage.

APPLYING FOR JOBS ONLINE

In an increasingly online marketplace, applying for jobs often means sending your résumé and cover letter electronically. Some companies have online application forms right on their Websites. Here, you can choose the job you wish to apply for, plug your work experience, skills, and education into online fields, then submit this information with a single click of a button.

Online application forms differ from another and will require different information. For example, some companies ask that you "copy-and-paste" your résumé and cover letter into two fields. Others ask that applicants fill in multiple fields such as "work experience," "education," etc. Still others ask that you do both—submit your résumé and cover letter, and fill in fields that require the same employment-related information.

Whatever type of online application form a company might have, be sure that *all* your information is posted in one field or another. Don't be afraid to repeat information, especially if the form requests a résumé and a separate breakdown of your work history. Your information will be automatically uploaded into an online database, where hiring managers will likely scout for keywords. The more times your keywords come up, the better.

While some companies—especially large ones—have online application forms, many others simply ask candidates to e-mail their application materials to the appropriate person or to a general employment address like "hiringmanager@anycompany.com." Here, caution is warranted. Be sure to send your résumé and cover letter exactly as the hiring manager requests. Some employers prefer that the résumé and cover letter be attached as separate documents (usually in a Text Only format or as Microsoft Word documents). Other employers want the cover letter to be in the body of an e-mail, but the résumé to be attached separately. Still others prefer that both the résumé and the cover letter be pasted into the body of an e-mail. For the latter, be sure that your documents are easy to read. Résumés, which have a rather complicated format, often look messy when they are transplanted into the body of an e-mail. Says recruiter Beth Camp: "If you e-mail a résumé, it has to look as good as a written résumé. I would advise sending a résumé both as an attachment and in the body of your e-mail." This is a good way to side-step a possible formatting fiasco. Another way is to send your résumé and cover letter electronically, then to send hard copies as well.

Some jobseekers opt to purchase domain names and to create their own Websites for the purpose of putting their résumés (and other application materials) online. The advantage of formatting your résumé using HTML and making it a static Web page is that anyone can see your résumé in its proper format simply by visiting your Website. Thus, instead of mailing or e-mailing your résumé every time you want someone to see it, you can simply give the interested parties the right web address and they can find it for themselves. An added bonus of having your résumé on a Web page is that you may attract the interest of recruiters and employers whom you hadn't even considered. To make downloading your résumé easier, you may want to include on your Website copies of your résumé in PDF (portable document format) and Microsoft Word files.

Unfortunately, there are downsides to putting your résumé on a Website. One downside is that your information becomes accessible to everyone, even unwanted visitors. For this reason, you should never disclose your home address, social security number, or any other personal information. Another downside is that not all hiring managers will go out of their way to visit your Website. Even if your résumé is only a click away, many hiring managers would nevertheless prefer that you mail or e-mail it.

In terms of how you send your application materials, it would be unwise to go against the explicit wishes of an employer. For example, don't send an attachment when copy-and-pasting is requested. Some companies shun attachments because they fear getting a virus, or because they don't have compatible software, or because they simply don't want to be bothered with the extra step of opening a document.

When assembling your application materials and putting them into an e-mail, don't fill in the "to" field until you are finished. It's all too easy to accidentally send a half-finished e-mail to a company, thus eliminating your chances of making a decent first impression, and most likely, of getting an interview. If you were asked to copy-and-paste your résumé and cover letter, be sure to scan the final outcome at least once for formatting problems, then to use a spell checker a final time.

If you are attaching your documents, be absolutely sure you are attaching the right versions (i.e., the company-tailored and updated versions) to the employer. Also, be sure that they are labeled in a professional way. One jobseeker laments his decision to save different versions of his résumé under headings like "Résumé for Strategic Sourcing Jobs." Says the jobseeker: "I was applying for three different types of positions. But I didn't want every prospective employer to know that. By labeling my outgoing résumés the way I did, I pretty much broadcasted the fact that I didn't have a clear career direction." Probably the best strategy for saving your résumé is to do so under your name only (example: Gillian L. Holden résumé) or under your name and the name of the company (example: Greenfield résumé from Gillian L. Holden). Be sure to say in your e-mail what you have attached, and also, what software you've used. For example, you might say in the body of your e-mail: "Please see my attached résumé in Microsoft Word version 2002."

Before a hiring manager even opens your e-mail, she should know exactly who you are and which job you are applying for. In the "Subject" line, write your name, the position name (and job number, if listed), and the contents of your application (example, "Gillian L. Holden résumé and cover letter for Executive Assistant Position").

If you've been referred to a position by another person, be sure to "cc" (carbon copy) or "bcc" (blind carbon copy) your reference when you apply. That is, add that person's e-mail to the "cc" or "bcc" field, which will enable that person to receive an exact copy of the e-mail you're sending to the hiring manager. The reason you want to "cc" or "bcc" your referrer is because you want to keep him in the loop. After all, if someone has offered to help you, he should know what stage you're at in the application process. (Note: Some e-mail programs don't offer "cc" or "bcc" fields, in which case you'll want to e-mail your reference separately.)

Finally, be sure to save a copy of your outgoing e-mail in your "Sent Mail" folder, just in case the e-mail doesn't go through and you need to send it again. For more information on e-mailing, see "The Unspoken Rules of Online Job Correspondence" on pg. 115.

USING YOUR NETWORK

While responding to dozens of job ads is a method many jobseekers employ, it is surely not the most effective one. In fact, Beth Camp says, "I have very little faith in blindly sending a résumé and a cover letter—doing so generally doesn't get you the job. What gets you the job is knowing somebody or being proactive in the right way, including getting on the phone and following up."

As noted throughout this book, using your professional network is essential to finding a job. In a best-case scenario, you will know an employee at each of your prospective employers, and that employee will personally refer you to a hiring manager. A referral by a well-regarded employee sends a strong signal to an employer that you are a candidate worthy of consideration.

And lest you think that you are the only person to gain by being referred, consider this: The referrers at many companies receive bonuses if their referred candidates are hired. Says a senior human resources consultant at an insurance company: "We do pay our employees for referrals. It's one of the most generous referral programs I've ever heard of. Employees can receive up to five thousand dollars simply by referring a friend or associate. Referrals are how we get the best candidates—because we have extremely high standards and the people who know this best are the people who already work for us. They wouldn't refer people they weren't confident about because their own reputations are at stake."

Using your network is important for another reason: Without referrals, you probably won't hear back from many employers—especially in a slow economy. Says Beth Camp: "If you're sending out résumés and cover letters blindly and not getting a response, that's normal. If you're using your network, the search can still take six months—depending on what industry you're going for." Indeed, even candidates who draw upon their professional networks regularly have to be realistic about the likelihood of a prolonged job search.

While some people will undoubtedly find jobs by sending their résumés and cover letters without any connection to the employer, smart jobseekers know that outwitting the job market may require a bit more ingenuity. Explains Camp: "If you're in an industry—and if you're well networked—you can usually get in through some other means than through the front door HR department."

THE IMPORTANCE OF FOLLOWING UP

Simply sending your résumé and cover letter only guarantees that they will sit in a database, perhaps untouched, for up to a year. Employers and recruiters alike stress that jobseekers must be diligent, direct, and determined when applying for jobs. This means networking. It also means following up with the hiring manager once you have submitted your application materials.

Approximately one week after you have sent your materials, call or e-mail the hiring manager to inquire if she has received them. You can also call to ask about the possibility of scheduling a face-to-face meeting—especially if you've mentioned in your cover letter that you intend to touch base on a certain date. Finally, at a company that is of specific interest to you, asking for an informational interview can't do any harm—even after you've already applied for a position there. Such persistence shows your commitment. Says an HR manager at a global information technology company: "We're looking for resilience. There are constant organizational changes and shifts [at our company]. We're looking for someone who won't get bogged down. Especially in a large corporation, resilience is essential because there is structure and it takes time for things to go through."

The "rule of three" can be applied to following up, as it was earlier in this book to cold calling. Try e-mailing, phoning, or writing a paper-based letter to the hiring manager once, twice, but no more than three times. If she does not respond to you by that point, she probably has another candidate in mind and will only be bothered by multiple inquiries. Says Robin Pelzman, a human resources specialist: "You have to think about who you're calling and why they would be receptive to you. While persistence is good, you may end up irritating someone by repeated calls to the HR department." However, Pelzman does note that in her career a few persistent candidates have caught her attention—especially when they displayed courtesy and respect. "Sometimes in the past I saw a candidate I liked but couldn't hire right away. I'd say, 'Don't call me now. Call me in two months.' If that person did call me back, I would be receptive. I would remember them, especially if they were professional and hadn't called me back until then."

RECRUITERS AND THE APPLICATION PROCESS

If you're working with a recruiter, the usual application procedures may not apply. Says recruiting expert Beth Camp: "If you're going to go through a recruiter, cover letters are pretty useless. Recruiters are in a position to bypass the need for a cover letter." Indeed, because many recruiters work directly with employers, typical gestures—cover letters, following up, etc.—are sometimes a moot point. If a recruiter agrees to represent you, she will likely be the link between you and the hiring manager—and she will be the one to guide you through the process.

Often, it's not a bad idea to use a recruiter, even if you're also planning on applying for jobs on your own. Recruiters may be able to open doors that would be locked to an unrepresented jobseeker. They're also first in line to hear about new openings, especially at companies they've worked with before. Recommends Camp: "[If you use a good recruiter,] stay in touch with them, and be pleasant and charming, so that they will think of you when a new position opens up." Also, be sure to ask what the recruiter expects of you in terms of procedure and what you can expect of her.

The Unspoken Rules of Online Job Correspondence

In the world of online correspondence, some rules are the same as in regular letter writing (politeness is always in style) while other rules are completely different (no need for postage!). Follow the suggestions below to ensure that your employment-related e-mails are in tip-top condition.

+ *Obey spelling and grammar rules.* E-mailing, which requires little more than some keyboarding skills and a decent Internet connection, sometimes seems immune from the rigors of proper spelling and punctuation, and even of regular sentence and paragraph structure. If you are e-mailing a friend, capitalizing proper nouns or inserting commas may seem like a bother. But with hiring managers, such inattention to detail can seem like laziness or even disrespect—and it can destroy your chances of getting an interview. When e-mailing a potential employer, therefore, be sure that your e-mail contains no spelling or punctuation errors, and that your sentences and paragraphs are formatted correctly. Avoid the casual tone that is the norm in many e-mail situations. And definitely stay away from emoticons, those playful strings of characters such as [:-)] or[;( ] that indicate emotion.

+ *Keep your e-mails brief.* Hiring managers are always wishing they had more time. Bombarded with inquiries about job opportunities in good economic times and bad, they often skim unsolicited cover letters and résumés—if they get to them at all. For this reason, jobseekers should make sure their e-mailed résumés and cover letters are as short as paper-based versions—and preferably even shorter. Remember, cover letters should never be longer than one page, and résumés should seldom be so.

✦ *Open and close your e-mails as you would paper-based letters.* Just because you are sending an e-mail, don't throw basic letter-writing etiquette out the window. Be sure to use a proper greeting and a proper closing. And don't try to substitute a casual greeting like "Hey there" for a formal one.

✦ *Delete unnecessary information.* If you are sending your cover letter in the body of an e-mail, you don't necessarily need to include the same information you would include in a paper-based letter. For example, there's no need to include a date because when a hiring manager receives an e-mail, the date—and often the time—are automatically listed. You don't need to include the employer's address either, since your communication is occurring via e-mail.

NOTE: You should send the employer your mailing address, however, just in case a hiring manager needs to send you a letter via regular mail. At the very least, your address should be listed on your résumé.

✦ *Don't send unrelated information.* Hiring managers often groan when they receive extraneous information along with cover letters and e-mails. They would prefer that candidates not send pictures from their last vacations, or links to their personal Websites, or just about anything above and beyond standard job application materials. Says the Chicago-based recruiter: "An HR guy I work with told me that he recently received an e-mail with an image of a dancing pink bear at the bottom. And this was from a candidate applying for a serious job—a management job. . . . HR people don't even like to receive e-mails with colored text or background images. Sure, those e-mails stand out, but not in the right way."

✦ *Don't send an e-mail from your present employer's e-mail account.* If you're working for one employer, but applying for a job at another, do not under any circumstances use your work e-mail account to send your résumé and cover letter. This is considered unprofessional and unethical since you are using your present employer's resources to gain access to another company. A prospective employer will think, "What's to keep this person from doing the same thing at *my* place of business?"

Use a different e-mail account such as your personal home account for the purpose of applying for jobs. Yahoo.com and Hotmail.com offer them for free. While you want to use a different e-mail account, make sure your e-mail address is not too quirky. It should sound credible and professional to potential employers. Avoid anything along the lines of batgirl362636@aol.com, badass-motorcycle-dude@yahoo.com, or love towaterski@snet.net—you get the picture. A simpler e-mail address with only a name, such as AlmaMariaGomez@emailstore.com, is a much better idea.

NOTE: Many e-mail providers allow paying subscribers to use multiple aliases for the same account—for little or no charge. Contact your individual provider for more information.

Preparing Your References

As you send out your application materials, start to think about the people you want to use as your employment references. If a hiring manager is interested in bringing you aboard, he will generally ask for three references who are familiar with how you are as an employee. These should be people who have worked with you in the past, preferably including your former supervisors. Using friends or family members as employment references is typically not acceptable.

"Giving references," says Beth Camp, "is like giving a cover letter—it's an expected part of the process. Your references are expected to be good." Indeed, many HR professionals assume that candidates won't give someone as a reference if they aren't already sure that that the person will provide stellar feedback. However, even if a person likes you and respects your working style, that person may not be the ideal reference if his communication skills are below par. Says Camp: "Some people just don't know how to give a reference. As opposed to being a mouthpiece for good, they can be a mouthpiece for mediocrity. They can say, 'Yeah, he did an okay job,' and then there is dead silence on the phone. The employer will think, 'Well, what does *that* mean?' Just one wishy-washy answer can sink you."

By the same token, a fraction of all references deliberately attempt to damage the credentials of the candidate in question. For this reason it's crucial to be absolutely sure that your references are trustworthy and well intentioned when it comes to your career. Camp estimates that bad references occur in approximately 5 percent of all cases—a small but significant number. She suggests circumnavigating the possibility of a bad reference by doing a phone test. "Never give a reference without being sure of what they'll say," she says. "A smart thing would be to have a person unrelated to you call the reference in order to check up on you."

Once you have chosen your references, you must ask them if they are willing to speak on your behalf. Being a reference is no small responsibility, as it involves fielding calls from hiring managers and speaking at length about a candidate's skills and abilities. Some people may not have the time or wherewithal to be a reference, so it's important to find this out early.

Once you have confirmed your references, the next step is to bring them up to speed. Says Robin Pelzman: "Pay your references the courtesy of telling them, 'This company may be calling you. Here's who they are and here's the position I'm applying for. I'd appreciate it if you could highlight the following things that I did.' You might also send them an e-mail with more details on what you'd like them to talk about. Most references appreciate such support, though not all will follow your suggestions. Also, don't leave your references hanging. Let them know what's going on with the position." You'll also want to make sure that your references' information matches yours. Beth Camp suggests confirming the information on your résumé against their memories of your employment. Make sure that they can answer questions about the dates of your employment, for example.

Lastly, try to line up your references well before you are asked in for an interview. A human resources advisor at a technology company says, "It's always nice to have references up front, so you don't have to ask." Be ready to present your interviewer with a reference sheet that includes your references' names, titles, company names, and complete contact information, including phone numbers and e-mail addresses. And make sure that the contact information is accurate: The same human resources adviser bemoans the number of times he has dialed an out-of-service phone number and used an e-mail address that is no longer valid. He adds, "From a hiring standpoint, it's positive for a candidate to give references up front, but only if those references are accurate, if the numbers are right, and the people are prepared for phone calls."

Key Chapter Points

✦ How you apply for a job is nearly as important as what you put in your résumé and cover letter. Follow the explicit wishes of each hiring manager, especially in terms of how you format and send your materials.

✦ When applying for jobs using an online application form, be sure to include all your relevant information, even if you have to repeat some portions in more than one online field. Your information may be automatically uploaded into an online database, where hiring managers will likely scout for keywords. The more times your keywords come up, the better.

✦   If you've been referred to a position at a company by an employee who works there, be sure to keep that person updated on your progress. Include him in any correspondence you have with the hiring manager. A referral by a well-regarded company employee tells the hiring manager that you are a candidate worthy of serious consideration.

✦   Following up with an employer after you have sent your application materials is crucial to advancing in the hiring process. Call or e-mail to ensure that the hiring manager has received your résumé and cover letter, and if possible, schedule an informational interview.

✦   When picking your employment references, be sure that they are articulate, enthusiastic, and trustworthy. Let them know up front which employers may be calling, which positions you are applying for, and what kind of employment information you wish for them to highlight.

Chapter Seven

PREPARING FOR
THE ALMIGHTY INTERVIEW

Once you've been invited for a job interview, it's tempting to think, "Well, if it goes well, it goes well. And if it doesn't, it doesn't." And while a blasé attitude is better than an excess of anxiety, keep in mind that interviewing is a skill. The more you practice, the better you'll become.

But how exactly can you practice for an interview? At the very minimum, you can revisit your Prospective Employer List and study the more recent news and developments of the company. It helps, too, to quiz yourself with questions you may be asked by your interviewer. Says former ESL instructor Kathleen Pierce, "[To prepare for interviews] I went over my résumé and I asked myself a few questions, such as 'What do you think your best qualities are?'"

But if you truly want to wow an interviewer, you'll probably want to go further than cursory preparatory work. After all, the interview is a make-or-break moment. The hiring manager has presumably read your résumé and cover letter and decided that you are someone worth meeting. But her opinion ends there. What will truly shape, sharpen, and inform her view of you is what you say in your interview, how you behave, and even how you dress.

The Best Ways to Prepare

To prepare for this encounter—"the half hour that can change your life," as one jobseeker calls the interview—you'll want to take a thoughtful and thorough approach. That means starting early—even before you've been invited for an interview. It also means trying the ideas below, which have been tested and approved by hiring managers, HR representatives, and other jobseekers alike.

RESEARCH THE COMPANY EXHAUSTIVELY

It's one thing to brush up on a company by reading its Website, and perhaps, one or two newspaper articles you've stumbled across. But it's something else entirely to research the company with tenacity and ferocity. Think about it from the hiring manager's perspective. Would you be more likely to hire the interview candidate who can provide a patchy understanding of the company or the candidate who can spit out specific facts with precision and self-confidence? Obviously, the latter candidate will be the person most likely to be offered a position, or at the very least, an opportunity for a second interview. One human resources consultant says, "I once had a phone screen interview where the candidate knew the number of people in our company. He even had a general understanding of how many people were in this particular office. How did he know that? I don't care—I was impressed that he knew it at all." That candidate was invited for a second interview.

One recruiter at a global consulting firm insists that "doing your homework and learning everything you can from the public domain are motions that anyone would want to go through." She says that candidates should spend as much time as it takes to be up to speed on all company news. In preparing your Prospective Employer List, you've likely already read a lot on the company where you'll be interviewing. You've probably scanned the official company Website, financial reports, business and career periodicals, career Websites, and more. Now is the time to not only revisit this information, but also to learn it—really learn it, the way a student would read, process, and ultimately memorize information before an exam. It's also the time to go back to these information sources to see if any new company developments have occurred since you first compiled your Prospective Employer List.

While it's crucial to learn about the company, you'll also need to learn about the job itself. When asked what kind of questions he prefers to ask interviewees, a human resources manager at an international IT provider says, "I like to ask, 'What's your understanding of the job?' Sometimes job candidates have a good idea and sometimes they don't. I like to know that they know what they're signing up to do. If they don't know quite what the job calls for, but they still think they're the number one person for the job, then there's an inconsistency." Indeed, how is a candidate supposed to prove that she can do the job if she has little clue what it entails? The best way to go about learning about the facets of the job is to reread—and ultimately memorize—the position description posted on the employment advertisement. Even better, speak with someone who works in a similar position, preferably at that company or at a company in the same industry. That way you'll get a real-life account of what such an employee does and needs to know day to day.

REVIEW YOUR TAILORED RÉSUMÉ AND COVER LETTER

In a strange way, you—as the interviewee—have an advantage over the interviewer. While you can learn as much as possible about the company, the interviewer has limited access to information on you. In fact, most of the time the only things he will know will be derived from information you have given him on your résumé and cover letter. For this reason, reviewing your application materials—your tailored applicable materials (the exact version you sent to a particular company)—makes sense. In fact, some of the questions your interviewer will ask you will probably come straight from your résumé. Questions like "Why don't you walk me through the important points of your work history?" and "Can you tell me more about your recent experiences at X company?" are common. What's great about reviewing your résumé and cover letter in advance is that you can fully prepare yourself for such questions. You don't have to think on the fly because you've already thought through and practiced your answers.

If you've been referred to the position by an employee at the company, be sure to check with your referrer to see what he or she has already told the hiring manager about you. You'll be able to prepare your answers accordingly.

KNOW THYSELF (INCLUDING YOUR KEY SELLING POINTS)

"There's the story," says a senior human resources consultant. "What would you do if you found yourself in an elevator with the president of the company in which you were interviewing? You would have thirty seconds to sell yourself. Well, I'm looking for a thirty-minute sell—you have to know exactly what you did in previous jobs and what prompted you to leave them. There shouldn't be a whole lot of figuring that out in front of me." The crux of this consultant's statement is "Know thyself." She and other industry experts say that you should know exactly why you want the position, why you're suited for it, and what your strengths and weaknesses are—all before you walk through the door and shake your interviewer's hand. The interviewee who has to mull over questions for long intervals of time and ultimately comes up with imprecise or roundabout answers will leave the interview with an invisible rejection label stamped across his forehead.

Says a consultant at a human resources consulting firm: "Before I was hired here, I had a couple of miserable interviews. The interviewers asked the question: 'Why do you do international management? How does it tie in with your future career plans?' I didn't have a very strong logic to back up my answers. I was unprepared and I think it showed. You need to be very clear, sharp, and focused on your story. Tell the story so many times that you internalize it. Companies can pick up inconsistencies in your approach and your thinking." The importance of having a clear understanding of yourself as a professional cannot be underestimated. Just as important is knowing your Key Selling Points.

Your Key Selling Points are those skills and aspects of your job experience that are most relevant to the position that you are interviewing for. They may be skills that are adaptable to different jobs and working environments. Or they may be skills that are rare or highly sought after by certain employers. They may even be softer skills like interpersonal skills.

Everyone has Key Selling Points, but not everyone is able to identify what they are. Your job as you prepare for interviews is to identify at least five or six of your own Key Selling Points (seven or eight would be even better) and to figure out how you can convey these selling points in an interview. When you are asked an interview question, you'll want to answer it in a way that showcases at least one of your Key Selling Points. Suppose, for example, that the following question was asked by your interviewer: "What kind of work environment would allow you to be most effective on the job?" Suppose, too, that you know that this company fosters a hands-off management style and that one of your Key Selling Points is that you are extremely self-motivated. Here, you would want to answer the question by citing this selling point (since it is applicable to the position and to the company), then give one or two compelling examples of moments when you displayed self-motivation at your previous jobs.

Bear in mind that you should prepare both your Key Selling Points and examples that back up your selling points in advance of an interview. That way, as the senior human resources consultant noted earlier, there won't be "a whole lot of figuring that out" while you're sitting face-to-face with a hiring manager. The answer to the question will already be in your head. All you'll have to do speak it aloud.

Bear in mind, too, that just as every person has Key Selling Points, so too does every person have weak spots. You'll want to make sure your selling points are relevant to the position for which you are interviewing, but you shouldn't *make* them relevant by bending the truth or by pretending that your weak spots are actually strong. A professional at a global consulting firm notes that when it comes to interviewing, you should "represent yourself as honestly and openly as you can. The worst thing anyone can do is to get into a job they're not qualified for."

LISTEN TO THE ADVICE OF YOUR REFERRER

If you've been lucky enough to be referred to a position by a person who works at the company, you'll want to capitalize on this connection. Because your referrer is already a company insider, he will most likely be well acquainted with the company culture. He may even know quite a bit about the department with which you're interviewing, how interviews are normally conducted, which questions are generally asked, and the personality of your interviewer.

Some referrers are willing to recommend a candidate, but don't like to become further involved in the hiring process, preferring to sit back and let the candidate take some initiative. Other referrers feel invested in a candidate they recommend, and want to make sure the candidate is as prepared as possible when it comes time for an interview. If you've been referred, you'll have to gauge how much or how little your referrer is willing to assist you. Be polite in your inquiries, and don't apply pressure if your referrer seems uninterested or withdrawn. After all, he has already done you a favor by referring you in the first place. You don't want to come off as a pest.

If your referrer does express interest in continuing to help guide your efforts, by all means take his tips to heart. And be sure to ask relevant questions. What you can expect from the interview? How should you prepare? What information on your résumé should you target? Is there any subject you should avoid in conversation?

One jobseeker was steered toward a job opening by an employee at a financial services company. That employee not only recommended the jobseeker for the position, but also prepped him for the interview. The jobseeker recalls, "He told me that the interviewer, who was the director of the department where I would be working, liked candidates who had worked for name-brand companies. Fortunately, I had worked for two high-profile employers. A couple times in the interview I dropped those names—always in context, of course—knowing that they would be of interest. I guess it worked, because I got the job."

PICK WHAT YOU'RE GOING TO WEAR IN ADVANCE

Clothes—they don't make a person. But they do make a first impression. And in many—if not all—industries, first impressions matter. Of course, different industries have different dress codes. Internet companies are renowned for their casual, dress-down culture, while investment banks require much more formal attire. No matter what kind of company you are targeting, however, you should make every effort to look polished and professional on an interview.

"Make sure your shoes are polished," recommends Robin Pelzman, a human resources expert. "Clean your nails. Knot your tie properly. Look crisp and clean. These are simple things, and they might not make or break your chances, but they do make an impression." She adds, "It's better to be slightly overdressed than underdressed."

If you have an interview scheduled, don't wait until the last minute to decide your wardrobe. Pick out your outfit several days in advance and try it on in front of a full-length mirror to make sure that it fits properly, that it is clean, pressed, and in fashion, and most importantly, that it is interview-appropriate. Go light on accessories and jewelry. Women should be especially careful about their outfits, since women's fashions are more diverse than men's, leaving more room for error. Avoid short hemlines, sandals or open-toed shoes, deep necklines, flamboyant colors, dramatic makeup, bare legs, and perfumes or strong fragrances. No matter who you are, if you have any doubts about the basic "dress for success" rules, ask someone knowledgeable to give you a second opinion. If your outfit is vetoed, you'll still have time to come up with a better alternative.

Being clothing-conscious may seem like a bother, but hiring managers tend to notice the candidate whose hair is askew or whose slacks are rumpled. "I'm in a conservative industry, and I have a special customer group that looks to see if shoes are shined," say a human resources consultant in the insurance industry. "They care if you've cared enough to prepare yourself for an interview."

FIND YOUR WAY AHEAD OF TIME

Are you traveling to a new place for your interview? If you are, then you'll want not only to get good directions, but also to test them out ahead of time. After all, nothing makes a worse impression then arriving late for an interview, sweaty and harried, with a story about heavy traffic, subway delays, or roadway construction. To avoid these scenarios, which hiring managers say they hear all too frequently, visit your destination once before your scheduled interview to verify and familiarize yourself with the route. Time how long it takes to get there, keeping in mind that traffic and public transportation conditions vary at different times of the day. If possible, also find an alternative route—just in case the unthinkable occurs (a pileup on the highway, a strike among railroad employees) and you need to reach your destination another way.

You should plan on arriving early to your interview, but not too early. Hiring managers say between five and ten minutes is fine. Coming too early, however, is a no-no as it may disrupt your interviewer's busy schedule and cause her to become irritated. By arriving too early you also risk seeming overeager for the job. It's better to wait out those extra minutes parked in your car or walking around the block. That way, you can walk in and introduce yourself to the receptionist ten minutes in advance rather than twenty.

DECIDE WHAT TO BRING—AND WHAT TO LEAVE HOME

When going to your interview, be sure to bring extra copies of your résumé. Four times out of five you won't need to use them. But it's always nice to have a few on hand, in case the company's copy has been misplaced or you are interviewed by more than one person. Of course, the résumés you bring should be same version you initially sent the employer.

Carry your résumés, as well as a small notepad and a pen for taking notes, in a professional portfolio or briefcase. Portfolios and briefcases should be a conservative color like brown or black. If you don't already have this type of carrying device, you can buy an inexpensive one at most office supply stores—or even borrow one from a friend. If you're in school, at all costs avoid toting your backpack, which is a hallmark of student life, not the professional world.

Common sense dictates that you should leave gum, candy, and cigarettes at home. But do bring your best manners. Using slang or curse words during an interview is a sure way to get your name scratched off a company's candidate list.

HOLD A DRESS REHEARSAL

One of the best ways you can prepare for an interview is to arrange a dress rehearsal—also called a mock interview. The dress rehearsal is a practice interview complete with all the trimmings: a mock interviewer, a ready set of interview questions, and optimally, a video camera (or at least an audio tape) that will record the event and allow you to see and analyze your interview behavior.

The dress rehearsal allows you to practice for an interview—without any "real life" pressure. You should dress and prepare as you would for a real interview. You should also know your Key Selling Points, be mentally prepared to answer a variety of interview questions, and know which questions you will be asking the interviewer.

If you're in college or graduate school, there's a good chance your educational institution's career services center offers mock interview opportunities. One senior at an Ivy League university says, "My interview was videotaped. One of the career center people was my interviewer, and afterwards, we reviewed the footage together. I saw some things I was doing wrong, but the career center guy gave me even more advice. He said I should keep my voice—my pitch and modulation—more level. I tended to speak with an upward inflection. Every time I answered a question it sounded like I wasn't sure of myself. So I've been working on that—how to keep my voice even-toned."

Another jobseeker in graduate school took advantage of a school-sponsored mock interview opportunity. He says, "Reviewing my mock interview on tape, I saw how nervous I looked. I didn't look the interviewer in the eye. I hedged a lot. Even my hands were shaking a little. Meanwhile, my classmate had also done a mock interview. He was almost too casual—sitting way back in his chair, talking to the interviewer like he'd talk to a good friend. I'm glad I got to see the takes of each of us because it gave me an opportunity to compare and contrast."

If you're not in school, it's just as easy to create a do-it-yourself dress rehearsal. All you need is a space with two chairs, a friend who can act as your interviewer, a little privacy—and preferably, media equipment. Shawn Jarrett, a manager, adds, "For my first job out of business school, I was lucky enough to have a good friend who was experienced and spent time helping me prepare. He sat me down and walked me through the gambit of questions I might be asked." Jarrett goes on to say that the experience was instrumental in terms of preparation for real interviews.

He points out that interviewees should pay attention not only to what they say, but also to how they say it. "Confidence is the main thing," he declares. "I've never seen a job that was rocket science other than rocket science. Every job is about common sense. You need to be articulate and you need to be consistent." Working on improving your confidence level during a dress rehearsal is a helpful and harmless way to prepare for actual interviews. An HR manager at an IT company reiterates the primacy of confidence in potential employees. "Three important factors I consider when interviewing: confidence, preparation and honesty, with confidence being weighted most," he says. For more information on confidence, see "Confidence versus Cockiness" in chapter 8.

Another thing to keep in mind when you are participating in a mock interview is being direct. How direct you are will be a result of how much preparation you do. If you've rehearsed in advance what questions you might be asked and how you can answer them, if you've considered how you can incorporate your Key Selling Points into your answers, and if you've managed to settle your nerves (see "The Interview: Quelling Your Nerves" in chapter 8), then chances are you'll have no trouble being direct. If on the other hand you've bypassed preparation and walked into your interview cold, you may end up talking in circles. Your interviewer will of course take notice.

Says an HR manager at an IT corporation: "There was one candidate who just wouldn't answer the questions. I had to rephrase a question, but he still avoided it, which was frustrating." Either this candidate was trying to hide something, or more likely, he simply didn't have a ready-made answer and couldn't come up with one on the spot. This is why dress rehearsals are so important. They allow you to test out your answers in a safe environment. They allow you to make and correct your mistakes ahead of time. Best of all, they allow you to see for yourself if you're answering the question in the right context. "Answer questions directly," reminds Jarrett. "Don't try to beat around the bush. You fall on your face when you go off on tangents."

Interview Questions: An Overview

It's impossible to be one hundred percent prepared for every question an interviewer might toss your way. But believe it or not, you can come pretty close. In fact, interviewers tend to ask the same types of questions, but with slight variations. Witness the "weakness" question. There are dozens of ways to ask it ("Describe a time in your work history when you didn't perform up to par." "In which areas do you most need improvement?" "Tell me about a time you made a mistake on the job and what you learned from the experience." "What aspect of your management style would you most like to improve?") Yet at the core of each of these variations is the same question: "What is your weakness?" The same goes for the "career goals" question. You may be asked "Where do you see yourself in five years?" or "What are your long-term career aspirations?" or "Explain to me where you see your career going." Of course, each of these queries boils down to the same basic question: "What are your career goals?" The bottom line is that the majority of questions that interviewers are likely to ask funnel down to a fundamental few.

CURVEBALL QUESTIONS

Fine, the majority of interview questions are predictable. But what about the minority? What about those zany curveball questions like "If you inherited twenty million dollars, how would you spend the money?" or "If you could enter a time machine and be transported to any place at any time, where would you choose and why?" If you've been on enough interviews, chances are you've happened across at least one weird or madcap question. It may have left you fretful and faint. It probably left you tongue-tied. But hiring managers say that's normal.

Explains an HR professional at a popular retail chain: "Most quirky questions are really psychological questions. And they are asked for one of two reasons: Either the interviewer wants to see how you react in a strange or uncomfortable situation, or they want to see if you can take a question that seems unrelated to the job and produce an answer that is [related]." The HR professional makes a good point. For every unusual question, there is often a more reasonable question behind it—and that question is "Do you have what it takes to get this job?" The interviewer wants to see if you can think on your feet and ultimately come up with an answer that is creative, but also telling. She may also be testing your personality, to see if you are the kind of person who is easily shaken.

If you are thrown a curveball question, don't answer immediately. Take a moment to collect your thoughts. See if there's a way to steer your answer toward the requirements of the job. One jobseeker who was interviewing for an HR assistant position said that he was asked, "If you could be any kind of animal, what would you pick?" He explains, "I was stumped at first. In fact, I almost started laughing out of nervousness. But then I could see from my interviewer's face that she was serious—or at least she was pretending to be serious. I told her, 'I would be an elephant because they are very intelligent and social animals and concerned with the well-being of the other elephants in their group.' These were qualities that professionals in HR have to have, so I think my answer was creative, but also germane, in a way." If you are asked a zany question like this one, know that there is no perfect response. Rather, the best you can do is keep calm and answer in a way that shows that you are imaginative, but also professional in a prickly situation.

LOGIC QUESTIONS

Another type of interview question is the logic question, also called the "brainteaser" or "problem-solving question." The logic question is generally used in fields like consulting and investment banking, although it is increasingly used in other industries. According to a 2003 investigative profile by National Public Radio, companies such as Microsoft, Boeing, and IBM are using logic questions with increasing frequency.

A sample logic question might be, "How many brand-new TV sets are sold in Atlanta each year?" You probably don't know the answer offhand—and an interviewer won't expect you to. Logic questions are typically geared not toward your ultimate response, but toward your approach. The interviewer wants to see how you break down the question and build an answer. This process involves considering what variables are at play. To solve the TV question, for example, you'd have to estimate the answers to a host of other questions: What is the population of Atlanta? Given this population, how many individual households exist? How many TVs does each household have? And what is average number of years a household keeps a TV before replacing it? If you were to determine these variables and others with some degree of accuracy, you would be able to form a reasonable response to the interviewer's question.

Keep in mind that there may not be one "right" answer and it seldom helps if you have inside knowledge (if you worked in a TV manufacturing factory, for example). What matters are your analytical and quantitative skills, your speed, and your level of creativity. Thinking aloud as you attempt to answer the question will help your interviewer to assess these criteria.

Not all logic questions require so much effort. In fact, some questions call for the simplest and most obvious responses. One strategy consultant remarks, "I was asked a classic brainteaser on one of my interviews—Why are manhole covers round?" He goes on to say that overthinking would have led to defeat. "The answer they wanted," he reveals, "is 'Manhole covers are round so that they don't fall into the manhole.'"

A great resource for logic questions, as well as other sorts of questions used in financial industry interviews, is Timothy Falcon Crack's book, *Heard on the Street: Quantitative Questions from Wall Street Job Interviews.*

CASE QUESTIONS

The case question is yet another kind of interview question. Case questions are usually reserved for people who have studied business administration at the graduate, and occasionally, the undergraduate level. If you're not in either of these categories, chances are you'll never come across case interview questions, so there's no need to prepare for them. The case question is, essentially, a question in which the candidate is asked to address the real or simulated business dilemma of a particular company. In a set time period, the candidate will usually have to assess the situation by identifying the key people and/or issues at stake, analyzing possible strategies, and offering a solution that is in keeping with the facts of the case.

Susan Cheng, a manager at a media entertainment company, says case questions are used to interview candidates in her department. "I usually give the candidate a case or two," she reveals. "These are mostly situations we've encountered in our work. We want to see how they handle cases from an analytical standpoint as well as how they are in dealing with people and how they'll fit into the culture." If you're unfamiliar with case interviews, but are entering a field like consulting where they are likely to be used in the interviewing process, be sure to learn more. Vault.com's *Vault Guide to the Case Interview* and Marc P. Cosentino's *Case in Point: Complete Case Interview Preparation,* both available on Amazon (www.amazon.com), are solid resources.

STANDARD QUESTIONS: TRADITIONAL AND BEHAVIORAL

Despite the many types of questions at the disposal of interviewers, most interviewees are likely to be asked standard questions only. Included in this standard category are traditional questions like, "What can you tell me about this company?" and behavioral questions. A behavioral question is any question that asks you to describe your actions in previous situations. The psychology behind behavioral questions is that candidates are likely to act in the future as they have acted in the past. Therefore, if you're asked a question like, "Tell me about an occasion when you acted on someone's suggestion," the interviewer will be using your answer as an indicator of how you might behave in the position for which you are interviewing. Both traditional and behavioral questions are asked in most interviews.

The Forty Most Common Interview Questions

A list of the Forty Most Common Interview Questions is below, but keep in mind that many other interview questions will be derived from these forty. When thinking about how you should answer each question, always consider how you can segue into one of your Key Selling Points. Consider, too, arriving at each interview with a mental list of creative ideas about what you would do in the position if you were hired, which one human resources manager says, "is a great way to impress just about any employer."

Remember that tact and discretion are of utmost importance in any interview. A common, but tricky question some interviewers ask is, "What other companies are you considering?" Here, you'll want to be honest, without revealing too much information or indicating to the interviewer that any other job is more appealing than this one. Other questions that will require lots of diplomacy—and as little negativity as possible—include, "Why did you leave your last job?" and "What would you do differently if you were in charge of this company?"

Finally, keep in mind that your interviewer's questions may not automatically educe the kind of information she needs to know. In the end, it is up to you—the interviewee—to provide enough details about yourself and your work experience that will satisfy that ultimate question: "Why should we hire you?"

1. What are your career goals?
2. How have your career goals changed over time?
3. If offered this position, how long would you plan on staying with our company?
4. What's your understanding of the job?
5. What could you bring to this position and to this company?
6. Why do you think you are more qualified than other candidates for this position?

7. Why do you want to work at this company?

8. What salary are you expecting?

9. What would you do differently if you were in charge of this company?

10. Name one of your weaknesses.

11. Name one your strengths.

12. Which areas of your work are most often praised?

13. Which areas of your work are most often criticized?

14. How do you think your last boss would describe you?

15. How do you think a colleague would describe you?

16. How do you think a subordinate would describe you?

17. Walk me through the important points on your résumé.

18. Explain to me how your work experience is relevant to this position.

19. Why did you leave your last job?

20. What other companies are you considering?

21. Tell me about your work style.

22. Tell me what your ideal job would be like.

23. What criteria do you use for evaluating success?

24. Do you consider yourself a leader? What qualities make a good leader?

25. Tell me about a problem you've encountered on the job and how you dealt with it.

26. Tell me about a situation in which you failed to resolve a conflict.

27. Tell me about an occasion when you acted on someone's suggestion.

28. Are you willing to travel for this job?

29. Are you willing to relocate for this job?

30. Describe a project that you're especially proud of. What was your role in this project?

31. Why did you choose your college major?

32. How do you spend your spare time?

33. How do you stay current or up-to-date in this industry?

34. Tell me about a time when you used your creativity to overcome a problem.

35. Which of your skills—technical or otherwise—has most helped you on the job?

36. What new skills have you learned or developed recently?

37. Have you made an oral or written presentation recently? Please describe it.

38. What else should I know about you?

39. What questions do you have for me?

40. Why should we hire you?

When It's Your Turn to Ask the Questions

Many interviewers wait until the end of an interview to ask that infamous question: "Do you have any questions for me?" For some candidates, that question brings on a sigh of relief. At last, the grilling is nearly over. It's time to turn the tables. Or is it?

A number of hiring managers say that the questions interviewees ask are as telling as the answers they give. If a candidate asks vapid, vague, or general questions, it's a mark against him. If a candidate doesn't have any questions at all, it's at least three marks. On the other hand, the candidate who asks one or more sharp questions can earn the respect of an interviewer and even save a mediocre interview from spinning into a black hole.

Below are some suggestions for what to ask and what to avoid when you're in the driver's seat.

WHAT TO ASK

"My advice to anyone going in for an interview is . . . to come with a set of questions. Base those questions on your homework," advises one consultant at prominent international firm. "For example, you might ask, 'I was reading your annual report and it looks like you were doing X, Y, and Z—can you tell me why?' or 'I was reading the bios of the board members and it seems like you have a lot of board members with this type of background—was that a specific choice?'" Indeed, choosing questions based on your research shows several desirable professional qualities: conscientiousness, preparedness, and an ability to extrapolate.

David Wittenberg, a manager, suggests taking a preemptive approach when it's your turn to ask questions. That is, he suggests guarding against problems before they actually arise. "A question I always like to ask is—'Do you have any reservations about me?' It's an extremely useful question at the end of an interview, especially if there are multiple candidates. It gives you a chance to discover any objections lingering in the interviewer's mind while you still have a chance to address and overcome them." Wittenberg also advises candidates to ask for a postmortem session, regardless of whether they get the job. By "postmortem session," Wittenberg means an after-interview meeting in which the interviewer gives the candidate feedback. Wittenberg says, "If I am chosen, I can use that meeting to confirm the manager's decision and start planning for the onboarding process. Even more importantly, if I am not selected, I can get constructive feedback on how to present myself better in future interviews."

Susan Cheng believes that it is in some cases appropriate to ask your interviewer his personal opinion about the job. "If it's a peer, someone who works in a similar position, then it's absolutely fine to ask, 'What are some of the things that you wish you would have known about your job?' It's a good substitute for the 'What is your day like?' question, which I think is not applicable for professionals in many industries," she says. Ben O'Connell, a producer at a major public affairs network, offers a similar slant: "During your interview, ask your interviewer, 'What is it like to work in the company?' Most of the time, even if the interviewer is not telling the whole truth, you can get some idea of what he or she is thinking. If they start talking about the company being high-pressure and intense, it probably will be very stressful and your quality of life might not be that good." Kathleen Pierce, a former educational instructor, says in past interviews she has been straightforward about asking her interviewers if they enjoy working for their companies. "In answering they sort of gave me a sense of who they are as people, which was important because I knew I would be working under them. I judged not only what they said, but also how they said it. I saw what they expected of me implicitly, rather than what the explicit job description indicated."

Below are some other questions that are appropriate to ask your interviewer.

◆ How long has this position existed and how often has it been filled in the last three years?

◆ What are the common attributes of successful employees in this department?

◆ What qualities would the ideal candidate for this position possess?

◆ With which employees will I be working closely?

◆ What opportunities exist for professional training and development?

◆ How do you measure the performance of your employees?

◆ What opportunities for advancement exist for the person in this position who exceeds company expectations?

◆ Can you tell me about the leadership style of the department head?

✦ What is the next step in the process?

✦ When do you expect to make your decision?

Beware of asking too many questions, however, because you don't want to badger your interviewer or take too much of her time. "You don't need [a ton] of questions," says one consultant, "just three or five good questions based on your research."

WHAT TO AVOID

When asking questions, you should be careful about avoiding a few areas that are the equivalent of interview quicksand. The first area is anything that the interviewer has already covered. While it's fine to verify a point that's been made or to cover a different facet of the same topic, don't assume ignorance and request the needless repetition of the same information. Says an HR consultant at a mutual insurance company: "I had a candidate come in recently. I had already spoken to him and gone through the whole dog and pony show regarding what we do. The candidate then spoke to a supervisor, who also went through an overview of the company, but the candidate didn't say that he'd heard the information before. Then the candidate talked to a manager and again he acted as if he were ignorant. These were back-to-back interviews, so it wasn't as if he had an opportunity to forget what he'd heard. My advice to candidates is to pay attention to what people are saying to you."

The HR consultant finishes by saying that "you should do your research before you come in." Indeed, anything that is readily accessible in the public domain—on a company's Website, for example—should not be fodder for your questions. For example, you shouldn't ask questions that are already answered by the information you've collected on your Prospective Employer List. However, it's perfectly reasonable to ask questions that are *related* to information that you've collected but that have not been directly addressed or answered by your research.

Hiring managers do not like to field questions about compensation or benefits either. These are issues that should be addressed at a later stage in the hiring process, preferably once an offer is on the table (see chapter 10). Candidates who ask about compensation or benefits on a first interview are only demolishing their own prospects. "If on a first interview the first question out of your mouth is, 'How much vacation time would I get?' or 'When is the next paid holiday?' you're through, cooked, done," admonishes one candid HR employee.

Outwitting a Tough Interview Question

No matter how much you prepare for an interview, there is always the chance that an interviewer will ask a question that will make you squirm in your seat. Below are examples of a few interview zingers— and how best to deal with them.

IF YOU'VE "JOB-HOPPED"

If you've been invited for an interview despite the fact that you've had six jobs in the last three years, chances are your interviewer is interested in hiring you—but also interested in hearing a sound explanation for your erratic work history. In recent years, especially in light of the Internet boom and bust, employers have been more tolerant of workers who have skipped from job to job because of layoffs, or relocations, or other forgivable circumstances. However, company disloyalty is certainly not something a potential employer wants to see in a candidate—and you'll have to have a better explanation than, "Other employers kept offering me more money. What else could I do but jump ship?"

One hiring manager says that staying at a company for one full year—at the very minimum—is important for jobseekers because they "have to show they've produced and that they're capable of integrity and company loyalty." If the damage is already done, though, and you've job-hopped for less than compelling reasons, all you can really do is accentuate the positive. The same hiring manager suggests telling interviewers about the positive aspects of your employment, rather than dwelling on the fact that you haven't been at any one company for long. Repeat your answer in a mock interview situation until you feel comfortable saying it. Try to convey that you are in fact willing and able to make long-term commitments. If you've been a long-standing member of a volunteer group or professional organization, for instance, you can use this information to bolster your case.

NOTE: According to a poll by the Society for Human Resources Management, the majority of HR professionals describe a "job-hopper" as one who changes positions once a year or even more frequently.

IF YOU HAVE HOLES IN YOUR WORK HISTORY

Having holes in your work history holds a similar stigma to job-hopping. If you've been invited for an interview, your interviewer is already interested in you for the job. However, she may have some lingering reservations about why you didn't work for months, or in some cases, years. It's best to nip these reservations in the bud, rather than let them fester in the interviewer's mind. It's possible that you became a parent and had to take time off to raise your children or that you were caring for a seriously ill relative, for instance. Both are reasonable explanations for a long-term absence from the workforce, although you'll need to do more than earn an employer's sympathy to get hired—and in fact, a self-pitying or apologetic tone is never recommended in an interview situation.

The best thing to do is to counter the negative information—the holes in your work history—with positive information. Show that you've kept busy and career-minded by doing freelance work, taking classes, volunteering, or committing yourself to community or consulting projects. If the skills you used in any of these situations are transferable to the job for which you are interviewing, that's even better. You'll also want to prove that you've kept current with changes in your industry through reading or course work. Finally, you'll want to show that these holes in your work history are behind you and that you are now prepared for a long-term commitment to an employer. As with job-hopping, you can show this commitment by indicating your dedication to previous pursuits, such as long-term volunteer work.

If you have been chronically unemployed because you couldn't find a job, that's a little harder to justify—but not impossible, say employers. As always, emphasizing the positive—or at least defusing the negative—is crucial. For more tips on what to do if outwitting the job market is taking much longer than you expected, see chapter 9.

IF YOU'VE BEEN FIRED

Your interviewer has asked the question you were dreading—why you were fired from a previous position. Your hands go clammy. Beads of sweat start to dot your forehead. Your first instinct is to lie, but you know you can't. Before you spout out random emotional justifications, take a step back and assess your options. You have several.

One way to tackle this situation is to use a forward-thinking approach. Answer questions regarding the firing briefly and with as few gory details as possible. But don't try to weasel out of the matter, as your interviewer will notice any sneaky tactics. The key is to step away from the past and to reserve most of your response time for the positive things you will bring to a future employer.

A second option is to balance bad news with good. Acknowledge that you've been fired, but put the incident into perspective. Convince your interviewer that the firing is one mark in an otherwise spic-and-span employment record. Do this by citing positive contributions you made on the job and by assuring the interviewer that your references can vouch for your mostly stellar track record.

A third way to respond is to graciously accept the blame. Be warned: You don't want to burden a prospective employer with a lengthy account of how you bungled your job. Rather, your main concern is diverting the blame from your previous employer. No interviewer likes someone who makes excuses. In fact, several HR professionals said that an interviewee who bad-mouthed a former employer or manager would be automatically axed from contention. By taking the fall, you'll be showing a measure of maturity and self-awareness. "Being fired is a negative that can be turned into a positive if you can admit your wrongdoing and that you've corrected the problem," says a senior human resources consultant at a mutual insurance company.

IF YOU'RE ASKED THE "WEAKNESS" QUESTION

The weakness question is the undoing of many an interviewee. Yet it's actually one of the easier questions to answer. In an interview, you can pretty much count on the weakness question—or some variation of it—being asked. You'll therefore want to prepare your answer in advance and to practice until it rolls off your tongue with nary a hesitation. The key to the weakness question, as seasoned interviewees will tell you, is to present your weakness as a strength. Says Leigh Wetzel, an online manager, "In most every interview I will say, 'I used to have a problem delegating because it would sometimes be easier and faster to do everything myself. I've since managed projects that have required ten to fifteen people to complete, and I am now completely comfortable with allowing people to do their jobs and helping them to manage their tasks.' The weakness—'not delegating' [actually shows my] strong work ethic—and it is quickly countered with 'I've since grown past it.'" Leigh's point is well taken. Presenting a former weakness that you've already turned into a strength is a great way to go, as it shows that you're willing and able to undergo self-improvement.

Another way to answer the weakness question is to point out a weakness that has no bearing on your employability, and thus, is mostly harmless. That's not to say that you should expound upon something completely random like how you're addicted to peanut brittle. Rather, cite a skill that you wish you were better at. Even though this skill shouldn't be one that you'd use on the job, it helps if you can show a commitment to improvement. If you're taking classes to brush up, for example, be sure to tell the interviewer.

Whatever you choose as your weakness, be sure that it is something that won't be of major concern to an employer. Never point to a personal issue ("My hygiene could be better"), an unsettling or regretful employment issue ("I never get along with my coworkers"), or worst of all, a criminal problem ("Well, there's my shoplifting habit..."). And be sure that you don't say, "I don't have any weaknesses." This answer will sound an alarm in your interviewer's head that you're bigheaded or lack self-awareness.

Above all, your answer to the weakness question should underscore the idea that you are essentially a great worker whose career has been filled with light and lauds.

IF YOU'RE STILL STUMPED

If the question your interviewer asks causes goose bumps to rise despite your preparation, you'll have to go with a secondary strategy. If you're good at reading people, you can first try to guess what the interviewer is looking for. For every question, an interviewer is trying to extract certain information. A question like "What should I know about you that isn't on your résumé?" is not an invitation for you to talk about your shoe size or favorite pizza topping, for example. Rather, it's a question designed for you to tout accomplishments or skills that aren't in your application materials. If you think you've decoded your interviewer's intentions, proceed—but with caution. Remember, you're not a bona fide psychic.

If reading people is not your strong suit and you have no idea how to respond to a question, buy yourself some time. Repeat the question aloud—or ask for clarification. You will probably give off an aura of poise. The interviewer will likely think, "This is a candidate who carefully deliberates instead of giving rash responses." Reflecting on a response shouldn't take you longer than a few moments, but that may be enough time to get on track.

If after a pause you still don't know how to answer, don't panic. Smile and keep breathing. Remember that how you react is as important as what you say. Mentally flip through your Key Selling Points and see if you can connect one to the question at hand. If you are still in a lurch, a last option is total candor. Admit that the question is difficult to answer and that you would like to go back to it later in the interview. At this point, your interviewer may take mercy on you, perhaps even pointing you in the right direction. If she doesn't, you can try an alternative response—one that has a positive spin. If the question focused on a poor reference, for example, you could say, "I don't know why that person gave me a negative reference. As you can see, my other references focus on my organizational skills, professionalism, and attention to detail. If you'd like, I can tell you why I believe those references to be more accurate."

No matter how you respond, don't let your anxiety grow to the point that it jeopardizes the interview. For ideas on how to quell your nerves, see chapter 8.

Key Chapter Points

✦ An interview requires extensive preparation that includes, but is not limited to, researching the company exhaustively, reviewing your tailored résumé and cover letter, knowing your Key Selling Points, and heeding the advice of your referrer.

✦ One of the best ways you can prepare for an interview is to arrange a dress rehearsal—also called a mock interview. The dress rehearsal will allow you to test out your answers in a safe environment, make and correct mistakes ahead of time, and to see for yourself if you're answering the questions in the right context.

✦ Your interviewer's questions may not automatically educe the kind of information she needs to know. It is up to you to provide details about yourself and your work experience that are relevant to the job opening. Preparing in advance your answers to "The Forty Most Common Interview Questions" will help you to steer conversation in the right direction.

✦ Hiring managers say that the questions interviewees ask are as telling as the answers they give. Be sure to come to your interview armed with a handful of insightful questions based on your research.

Chapter Eight

THE INTERVIEW: MAKING IT WORK

Give yourself a hand. If you've been invited for an interview, you've already jumped some significant hurdles in your quest to outwit the job market. But another hurdle looms ahead. Your interview is not simply an exchange of information. Your interviewer, as an ambassador of the company, is testing your personality, knowledge and experience, and potential fit within the organization. You, in turn, are selling yourself as a candidate and evaluating the company as a potential employer. In order to set yourself apart from competing job candidates, you've got to stay on your toes while remaining calm. Here's how.

The first thing to remember about an interview is that it's a time for mutual evaluation. You have as much right to assess a potential employer as that potential employer has to assess you. Shawn Jarrett, a manager, says, "I'm not necessarily going to go for a job just because you're offering it. My advice to jobseekers: You have to fit the job and the job has to fit you." Jarrett's point is valid. It's best to find a job that is compatible with who you are and how you work. Sometimes that compatibility—or lack thereof—is apparent from the outset. Jarrett remarks, "When you first meet someone you get a feeling about them—a gut feeling. You should always stick with that feeling—it should be your guide for better or worse." Leigh Wetzel, an online manager, believes in the benefits of evaluating your employer. "Remember you are also doing the interviewing," she advises. "Desperation aside, you have to ask yourself, do I want to spend fifty or sixty hours a week at this place? Is there long-term comfort here? Personally, I like to know what kind of support I will get in a position."

"Fit" is important to employers too, and some place the highest premium on it. Says one senior human resources consultant: "Fit is really the number one thing here. We feel that if you're the right person, we can teach you the skills. If you have the drive, the focus, and the ambition to learn, that might get you farther than someone with twenty years of experience."

The second thing to remember is that interviews require a degree of salesmanship. You'll have around thirty minutes to convince an employer that you're the right person for the job, so make the most of that time. In the previous chapter, you worked out answers to the Forty Most Common Interview Questions, took stock of your Key Selling Points, exhaustively researched the company, and created a few thoughtful questions of your own. Now you'll take the next step. You'll have to tout your skills and experience—all you've done and all you're capable of doing—in a way that hooks the employer. Put yourself in the interviewer's shoes and try to present information that is applicable to the company in general, and to the position in particular. You might have the best work experience in the world, but it won't count for much if your interviewer doesn't think it pertains to the job. In some cases, you may have to relay information independently of the questions asked. It's perfectly fine to say, for instance, "We haven't discussed my experience in business development, which I think is very relevant to the demands of this position. I'd like to tell you about it."

Thirdly, remember that the success of an interview is contingent upon preparedness. If you've followed the steps in chapter 7, you're already more prepared than most candidates with regard to what to expect during an interview. Now familiarize yourself with the various interview formats.

Interview Formats

THE ONE-ON-ONE INTERVIEW

The one-on-one interview is by far the most common type of interview. It usually takes place on-site—that is, at the company location. You will interview with one person, usually the person who would be your direct supervisor or manager. You may also speak, in separate one-on-one interviews, with the head of the department or with a human resources representative for the company.

THE PANEL OR COMMITTEE INTERVIEW

The panel or committee interview, which most often takes place on-site, consists of a group of people who interview you en masse. The panel interview is often more overwhelming than the one-on-one interview because you will have to concentrate on two or more people, each of whom may have a different interviewing style. During the panel interview, maintain eye contact with the person asking the question, but attempt to give each interviewer an equal measure of your attention.

THE PHONE INTERVIEW

The phone interview is increasing in popularity, especially as a screening device, or as a way to weed out unwanted candidates before the start of the regular on-site interview process. Phone interviews require an adjustment in behavior, as your emotions will be read through your voice, rather than through gestures or facial expressions. Make sure to speak your answers slowly and deliberately, so that the interviewer will be able to understand you. Keep notes and your tailored résumé handy so that you will remember all the points you wish to make. Be sure to speak in a quiet room where there are no distractions—a ringing doorbell or a droning radio or television will throw off your concentration, and perhaps, irritate your interviewer. To avoid static or a bad connection, consider using a regular phone rather than a cellular or portable phone. Also keep in mind that the rhythm of your conversation may be different than in a face-to-face situation. Your interviewer may be taking notes as you speak, leading to gaps in the conversation.

In scheduling a phone interview, remember that your interviewer may live in a different time zone, and thus, have an interview time that varies from yours. Also remember that the message on your answering machine or voicemail is a reflection of who you are. A casual, silly, or unduly long message will probably strike an interviewer as unprofessional. Another phone interview "don't" is eating or chewing gum while you speak. "It's about the worst thing you can do," remarks one human resources professional.

It's often hard to be yourself during a phone interview because of the miles of cable separating you from your interviewer. A senior graphic designer gives this suggestion: "My phone interviews have generally been twenty to thirty minutes. The best advice I would give is to try to prolong it, so that the recruiter has made a connection with you and will want to hire you. Try to stay upbeat and enthusiastic so the recruiter will come away from the interview and remember you." If you have any doubts about how you sound, consider doing a practice run. Ask a friend to be the interviewer during an on-the-phone mock interview, then ask your friend for feedback on your performance.

THE GROUP INTERVIEW

The group interview can be one of two types. In the first instance, the group interview will be much like a panel interview. A team of people—often the same team that works together on company projects—will interview you collectively. In this case, you may be fielding questions from professionals at different levels of the company, even employees who may be your peers or subordinates. No matter who's asking the questions, be sure to treat everyone with respect and courtesy.

In the second instance, you may be placed with other interviewees and asked to answer questions or to solve a problem as a group. In this scenario, employers will be evaluating your behavior, knowledge, teamwork skills, and creativity against the other candidates. Here, you'll want make your mark and impress the employer without usurping power, or worse, showing no leadership ability at all.

THE STRESS INTERVIEW

The stress interview is an interview in which the interviewer deliberately attempts to make you uncomfortable, agitated, or even angry. Without notice or advance warning, she may ask untoward questions or respond to your answers in a mocking or acerbic way. Ugly as it may be, the stress interview is designed to see how you will react in a thorny situation. Keep in mind that everything an interviewer does may be designed to disturb and distress you. She wants to see if you can maintain your composure through the antagonism and still answer the questions in a professional way.

Stress interviews are not common, nor are they pleasant, but they are always memorable. Be sure to keep your cool. Even if you are want to chastise the interviewer for provoking you, refrain from doing so. You will fail the stress interview if you let your acrimony show.

THE LUNCH OR DINNER INTERVIEW

The lunch or dinner interview is most often a one-on-one situation, although some lunch or dinner interviews may include two more interviewers. Some jobseekers think that a mealtime interview will be more casual than an on-site encounter. However, this is seldom the case. Says Eric Thompson, a programmer, "I interviewed with ten people for my job and the interviews ranged from one-on-one scenarios to four-on-one. At the end of the session there was a one-hour lunch, which I thought was going to be casual. But during that lunch everyone had a list of questions. They kept me on my toes."

While food is a great icebreaker in an interview situation—and talk of an especially tasty guacamole dip can fill an awkward silence—common sense should prevail. Order a dish that's in the same price range as what your interviewer is ordering (remember, she'll be paying). Make sure your food is easy to cut and chew (you don't want to have to wear a lobster bib), and avoid onion and garlic at all costs. If you're asked to order first, pick a dish that's in the medium price range. If possible, eat at the same pace as your interviewer—and order coffee and dessert only if she does. The same goes in spades for alcoholic beverages.

Remember, your interviewer may have opted for a mealtime interview in order to see how you act in a social situation. Make sure your table manners are tip-top. And be nice to the wait staff—your interviewer will notice.

THE VIDEOCONFERENCE INTERVIEW

The videoconference interview, which is fairly rare, is most often used if you cannot make it to an on-site interview, will be telecommuting to work, or if one or more of the interviewers are off-site. The videoconference interview, which has a variety of other names including "remote-access interview," provides the transmission of audio and video between two locations. Because the camera can catch you at only one angle, be sure to convey your enthusiasm through your words. Excessive gesturing and less-than-conservative attire can be distracting, so be sure to avoid both.

Access to videoconferencing equipment is necessary, and the company will provide you with information on the venue if this type of interview is requested. Be sure to arrive to the location at least thirty minutes early so that you familiarize yourself with your surroundings and make sure that the connection to your interviewer is working. One video-conference interviewee suggests aligning the camera and the monitor so that you can look at the latter without constantly turning away from the former. The same interviewee also suggests preparing yourself for small delays. The transmission may take several seconds to reach each party, giving the impression of delayed reactions. Be ready for this possibility and don't worry yourself over it.

Don't forget to sit straight in your chair and refrain from mumbling to yourself between questions. The camera will pick up errant talk and behavior. A great way to prepare for videoconference interviews is to videotape a mock interview. See "Hold a Dress Rehearsal" in chapter 7.

From Greetings to Follow-up

From the beginning of your interview until after you bid good-bye, it's essential to pay attention to the messages you're sending your interviewer. These include obvious responses, such as the content of your answers, to more subtle communications like your mannerisms and speech patterns.

THE IMPORTANCE OF BODY LANGUAGE

SHAKE HANDS THE PROPER WAY

One of the first things you'll probably do in an interview is shake hands with your interviewer. The handshake is a simple symbol of introduction. But it can also be an unspoken gauge of personality. Hiring managers say that while a limp or unenthusiastic handshake won't destroy an interview, it can cause one to start off on a bad note. The same goes for a sweaty palm. To alleviate the latter problem, be sure to keep your hands open, not balled into fists, prior to your interview. This will reduce perspiration. Put a handkerchief or a few tissues in your pocket, just in case. Also remember that while a limp handshake is bad, a bone-breaking handshake isn't much better. Clasp your interviewer's hand firmly and confidently, but don't overdo.

MAINTAIN EYE CONTACT

A lack of eye contact during an interview can lead your interviewer to think that you're shy, disinterested, or dishonest. Likewise, shifting your eyes to and from the interviewer's face can also send the wrong message. It's no wonder "shifty-eyed" is a term used to describe a character who is deceitful or insincere. While you don't want to stare at your interviewer to the point making him uncomfortable, do maintain eye contact as much as seems appropriate. If you are speaking to more than one interviewer, you *can* shift your gaze, but be sure to look each interviewer in the eye for at least a couple of seconds.

WATCH YOUR BODY LANGUAGE

The term "body language" includes just about any manner, gesture, or posture that conveys meaning to the observer. Body language is especially meaningful in an interview as your interviewer will be paying attention to nonverbal cues as much as to what you have to say. Body language to avoid in an interview includes repeatedly crossing and uncrossing your legs or arms, fiddling with your hair or clothes, touching your face, scratching your head, or playing with a button or pen. Constant or bold gesturing is also to be avoided. Some of these mannerisms may be triggered by nervousness. Interview preparation and rehearsal may help you to feel more relaxed (see chapter 7). For more tips on stress relief, see "The Interview: Quelling Your Nerves" on pg. 164. Body language that might give your interview a boost includes leaning forward slightly to show your enthusiasm and nodding whenever is appropriate, particularly when your interviewer is making an important point.

SMILE WHEN YOU MEAN IT

Smiling, the universal sign of happiness, is a great way to convince your interviewer that you're genuinely pleased to be there. On the other hand, an oversized or artificial grin used too often during the interview will lead to the opposite result. Your interviewer will know you're forcing yourself to act a certain way.

According to *Discover Magazine,* when a person is sincerely amused, a part of the brain called the basal ganglia is activated, leading to the unconscious contracting of certain facial muscles. A forced smile, however, uses a different group of muscles, which is why it's generally easy to spot a person who is legitimately pleased from one who is only pretending to be.

During an interview, be sure to smile—but only when you mean it. It's infinitely better to smile occasionally but earnestly than to smirk constantly for no reason at all.

Be Mindful of Personal Space

Individual cultures—and even individual people—have different interpretations of what constitutes an appropriate amount of personal space. While one person might feel at ease speaking only inches from someone's face, another person might need several feet of separation. When facing your interviewer, be mindful of how close you stand or sit. Try to maintain a distance of about three feet. Communicating at a closer range may cause your interviewer to feel uncomfortable. On the other hand, sitting or standing too far away is also impolite.

OTHER MODES OF COMMUNICATION

Be Nice to Everyone

It's a no-brainer that you ought to be courteous to your interviewer, but what about the other employees you may encounter as you make your way through the interview process? Be very nice, say hiring managers, who have seen firsthand the repercussions of uncouth behavior. Susan Cheng, a manager at a media entertain company, says, "We've had candidates who were rude to the administrative assistants. Don't do that. You have to treat everyone the same way. We may ask the same administrative assistant who fell victim to a job-seeker's temper to conduct the callback to say, 'No, you didn't get the job.'" Now that's justice.

FOLLOW UP THE RIGHT WAY

What happens after the interview, after you've answered questions and made your case? According to one hiring manager, there's a right way and a wrong way to wrap up the event. The wrong way? To stumble awkwardly out the door with nary a look back. The right way? A confident handshake, a smile of appreciation, and a "thank you," for starters. Don't forget to ask for your interviewer's business card. It's a gesture of strong interest. It's also a practical move, as you'll want to have the interviewer's correct name spelling and job title for when you write your thank-you note.

And speaking of thank-you notes, you should send one as soon as possible. Melissa Walker, an associate editor, says, "Always write a hand-written thank-you the day after your interview. I interviewed interns at the magazine where I worked, and the ones who wrote me thank-yous put themselves ahead." She cautions against sending e-mail thank-yous, although an e-mail is better than no follow-up. "Sending an e-mail thank-you doesn't hurt at all—it's fine—but it doesn't show the same level of respect," she stresses. "It helps more than not sending one at all, but it's too easy. A proper, written thank-you can just be a little note. It doesn't have to be a crazy Hallmark card, and in fact a crazy Hallmark card might cause you to lose points."

So what should you include in your thank-you note? In ten lines or fewer, be sure to reiterate your interest in the position, as well as your most applicable skills and experience. Underscore your ability to meet the challenges of the job, especially if your interviewer has raised any doubts about this issue. Last but not least, thank the interviewer for her time and consideration, and let her know how much you'd like to contribute to the team.

NOTE: If you've interviewed with more than one person at the company, send a separate thank-you to each person. Be sure to vary the contents of each card, though. Coworkers have been known to compare and contrast.

Be Aware of Your Conversational Habits

Even eloquent speakers sometimes display bad conversational habits during interviews. It's easy to become nervous and to jump from thought to thought without ever finishing the original point you were making. It's also easy to interrupt the interviewer as she is speaking in order to convey your own ideas. Fortunately, these lackluster conversational habits can be curbed with practice. The most effective way to ensure proper conversational etiquette is to videotape yourself during a mock interview and to assess, and, if necessary, alter your speech habits. For more information on mock interviews, see "Hold a Dress Rehearsal" in chapter 7.

Show Poise as You Wait

After your interview and after you've sent a thank-you, you may have to wait days, weeks, and in rare cases, even months before you hear back from the employer. While this wait time can seem like an eternity, don't lose your cool and hound your interviewer for an answer. Seeming overeager can trounce your chances of getting an offer.

If two weeks have passed since your interview, it's fine to follow up with one letter, e-mail, or phone inquiry. But don't stalk your interviewer if you don't hear back from her immediately. Says Cheng: "Sometimes candidates will call every five minutes to catch you live rather than leave a voicemail message. But just because a person isn't answering, doesn't mean they're not at their desk. It's better to leave your e-mail address in your first voice message and to say, 'You can respond at your convenience.'"

What We're Looking For: Tips from the Interviewers Themselves

It's all fine and well to wax poetic about the interview process, but what do the interviewers themselves want? Below, interviewers from different industries break their silence and reveal to jobseekers the secrets to getting hired.

A POSITIVE ATTITUDE

An HR manager at a federal judiciary pauses for a moment before explaining that he cares less about a candidate's skills and experience than he does about her outlook. He says, "The number one thing we are concerned about—because we have so many qualified people who apply—is, are we sure this person will have the right working attitude? We just spend [so] much time with each other, in meetings and discussing things, that we don't have time for people with a bad attitude." In other words, if a hiring manager has to choose between two equally qualified candidates, the person with the most cheerful disposition will likely win out. It makes sense. After all, who wants to spend forty or more hours a week with a killjoy?

An HR manager at a global IT provider offers similar testimony. "It comes back to confidence, energy, and a positive attitude," he proclaims. "I had interviewed candidates a little while back for a senior strategy position. One person had such energy, such passion. We needed a go-getter. It was the energy and passion that impressed me." It's little surprise that this jobseeker was offered the job.

A positive attitude is reflected in not only what a candidate says, but also what he doesn't say. Shawn Jarrett warns interviewers not to take an aggressive or superior attitude during interviews. "You don't want to interview the interviewer," he warns. "Don't ask too much into an interviewer's background—everything you ask should be directed toward the job or to ascertaining information on [your potential boss's] management style. Don't try to nitpick, or to try to find flaws in what people are saying. And even if you do, pointing them out will only make you lose points. Interviewers, like everyone else, don't want to be made to feel unintelligent."

HONESTY

Hiring managers say a startling number of candidates misrepresent themselves on interviews. Prospective employees may exaggerate parts of their work history or disguise aspects of their personalities. The occasional candidate will even out-and-out lie. Yet it is the straightforward candidate who is most appreciated by hiring managers.

Robin Pelzman, a former human resources specialist at Hewlett-Packard, says, "There are those lucky moments when, within the first five minutes, you know you've found the right person. This happened later in my career, when I'd built up my experience and I knew exactly what we needed in terms of fit. One person was memorable for his openness. He said, 'I have three other offers. Here are the amounts they're offering, but I want to work for HP. This is where I'd like to be.' His openness wasn't presented as 'I'm hot, so you'd better come after me.' It was presented as 'My values and work goals correspond with *this* company and I want to work *here*.' By being open about his preference for HP, he impressed me and made me far more receptive to his other attributes. Also, openness and honesty were valued at HP, so his demonstration of these qualities also made him stand out."

Indeed, Hewlett-Packard isn't the only company that values honesty in its employees. Hiring managers everywhere say that this quality is an essential. A consultant at a firm specializing in executive placements and board director appointments says that candidates should avoid practicing their answers as if they are memorizing lines because interviewers want to see natural self-expression. "I don't do a lot of prepping with my candidates because I want the interview to be an organic experience," she declares.

THE RIGHT EXPERIENCE

Work experience is often the first thing hiring managers look for when they peruse a résumé. They ask themselves, "Where did this person work? What did he do? And is his experience transferable?" Susan Cheng offers this nugget of wisdom on the topic: "In my area of work, we look at experience primarily. I'll glance at education, but for the most part, it comes down to the type of work experience and whether it's applicable." Cheng goes on to say, "We do project work, so we hire a lot of ex-consultants. . . . We definitely notice candidates with name-brand companies on their résumés. If we know a candidate has already worked for a company like Procter and Gamble, Motorola, or Intel, we know that the candidate has already gone through a rigorous screening process with a company with similarly high expectations."

Yet it isn't enough to have worked for the right kind of company. Name brands can only go so far, especially if you are under- or overqualified for the job. Explains Cheng: "In looking through résumés, I pay attention to whether the job a candidate is applying for is a lateral or promotion-based move. I'm skeptical when someone applies for a position that has declining responsibilities. Someone who is overqualified will get bored and they'll have different expectations. Nevertheless, sometimes we will make offers to 'overqualified' individuals, but in those cases, we want to know, 'Why do you want to work here and what kind of skills will you gain from a lateral or a lower move?'"

The HR manager at a federal judiciary echoes this sentiment. He says that too much experience—or too little—can cost a candidate a job offer. "If we are hiring entry-level clerks," he explains, "we may get 375 applications for temporary positions—these are three-year positions. In this case, we tend to look for people who do not have a lot of job experience. And the reason for this is that we are going to ask them to do a lot of grunt work, entry-level-type work such as filing. Someone with fifteen years of experience at a downtown, high-profile law firm won't be happy doing that. We just hired five people at the entry level. All have the same kind of profile. All are college graduates with a decent academic record and either a very small amount of work experience in a related field or a postgraduate paralegal certificate. The theory is that these people are going to be thrilled to have their first real jobs that give them vacations, a 401(k) type of plan, health insurance benefits, tuition reimbursement, and a very nice physical environment to be in."

GREAT OBSERVATIONAL SKILLS

Hiring managers say that many candidates are prepared for their interviews, but unprepared for questions that are asked out of turn. Yet in this ever-shifting job market, ingenuity and an ability to improvise are valuable assets in an employee. Explains Cheng: "[At my company] one candidate had to interview with about eight people. I was interviewer number six. I said, 'You've already interviewed with five people. Tell me what you think the culture is like here.' He was able to articulate it pretty well. Candidates frequently ask that question—'What is the culture like?'—at the end of the interview, so it was good that he had already assessed that." Hiring managers in all industries approve of the candidate who can both keenly appraise a situation and articulate what he sees.

CURRENT EMPLOYMENT

Even if you've had it up to your eyeballs with your present job, hiring managers advise that you keep working as you search for new employment. Why? Employers are often more interested in hiring candidates who are presently employed than those who are out of work. Beth

Camp, the owner of a professional placement service, says, "Go with market value for your skill, suck it up, and stay working." In other words, think twice about leaving your job if you don't have another already lined up or if the job market is stormy. But if you're already out of work, don't sweat it. Employers can—and often do—sympathize with people who have been unemployed for several months or more, especially when the economy is ailing.

The Interview: Quelling Your Nerves

When it comes time for an interview, it's only natural to feel a few butterflies in your stomach. Yet too many butterflies may signal excessive panic or anxiety, which are interview hazards, as hiring managers are looking for candidates with confidence to spare. If you find yourself sleepless the night before your interview, if the thought of facing your interviewer makes your head pound, or even if you're just mildly nervous, be sure to try the stress-relieving tips below. (Note: For information on relieving stress through thorough interview preparation, see chapter 7.)

KEEP YOUR INTERVIEW IN PERSPECTIVE

If you are out of work or are struggling financially, you may feel desperate for a job, and this desperation may be most acute before and during a job interview. Yet overemphasizing the importance of an interview will not help you to be a better interviewee. In fact, it may have the opposite effect. An overdose of worry is more likely to tarnish and weaken your interview performance. Therefore, it's best to put the interview in perspective. Recognize it for what it is—a good opportunity—and try to be optimistic about your chances. After all, you've already been invited to meet a hiring manager, which is—in and of itself—a validation of your employability.

Even if you don't get the job, other interviews will eventually come down the pipeline. And at the very least, you can use this interview to learn more about the process in general. Says Shawn Jarrett, a manager:

"There is nothing better than going on interviews for jobs that you probably won't get. It will give you the chance to hear and perfect the answer to the questions that you will hear over and over again while interviewing. Going on these types of interviews will help you to hone your story, to master the spin on the rough spots in your résumé. If you talk to enough people . . . about the same topic, things will start to gel. Something that sounded like a negative before will sound like a positive because you have found a way to spin it."

EAT WELL AND EXERCISE

Stress levels can be linked to your level of fitness. Therefore, it's important to be health conscious in general, but especially in the days and weeks leading up to your interview. Eat a variety of wholesome, nourishing foods and drinks, and refrain from those with "empty calories" like candy and soda. Sugar and caffeine can boost already high stress levels. Before an interview, keep things like chocolate, tea, and coffee to a minimum.

On the day of your interview, be sure to eat a well-balanced breakfast with foods like oatmeal, fresh fruits, egg whites, and yogurt. If you have time, try to exercise—even if it's just a brisk twenty-minute walk. Physical activity can flush out stress and drain accumulated tension. It can also boost your level of energy.

TRY BREATHING EXERCISES

Breathing—something you do naturally and unconsciously all the time—is one of the best anxiety relievers out there. Stress and breathing patterns are related and each can influence the other. By practicing long, deep inhalations and slow exhalations, you may be able to control your anxiety. Even ten deep breaths can work wonders.

Stress-busting breathing techniques can be learned and improved upon. Ask your favorite bookseller which titles on this topic come recommended. Check with your local community center, too—it may offer a stress management workshop that includes breathing control instruction.

Breathing, yoga and meditation can be soothing for those who feel frazzled. Consider investing in books or videos on these subjects, or if possible, visiting a yoga or meditation center.

GIVE YOURSELF A PEP TALK

It may sound clichéd, but you can be your own best friend or your own worst enemy. While a family member or good chum may give you the encouragement you need to sail through an interview, you can work the same magic on yourself. Each person has an internal dialogue running through his head. Before an interview, this dialogue may take a turn for the worse as reservations and personal fears mount.

Fortunately, you can keep upbeat if you remind yourself of the positive aspects of your situation. Remember that the employer must consider you worthy in order to have extended an invitation for an interview. Remember that you have researched the company and prepared yourself for all sorts of questions—this should give you confidence. Finally, try to rid your mind of doubts and worries. If your thoughts are self-affirming, you'll stand a much better chance of staving off stress.

RUN THROUGH THIS CHECKLIST OF INTERVIEW BASICS

Probably the best way to sidestep stress is to be so prepared for the interview that you leave nothing to chance. Run through the following checklist to make sure that you haven't forgotten any interview prerequisites.

1. Are you well-groomed and dressed in an interview-appropriate outfit?

2. Do you have tested-and-approved traveling directions?

3. Will you be ready to arrive to the interview a little ahead of schedule?

4. Do you have several copies of your tailored résumé printed on quality paper?

5. Do you have a copy of your references?

6. Are you carrying a small notepad and a pen in a professional portfolio or briefcase?

7. Do you have the name of your interviewer—and do you know how to pronounce that name?

8. Have you reread the job description?

9. Have you committed to memory the questions you want to ask the interviewer?

10. Have you reviewed your Key Selling Points a final time?

11. Have you turned off the ringer on your cellular phone?

If you've answered "yes" to each of these questions, you're ready to go.

Multiple Callbacks: Why an Employer May Invite You for a Second, Third, or Even Fourth Interview

Often a company will invite you for a second interview to ask a few more questions, clarify some information, or introduce you to other members of the team. Says an HR manager at a California-based IT headquarters: "At my company, usually there is a team of people interviewing. Some interviewers are [looking] for technical expertise, others for personality and fit. The second interview might be someone following up on a particular question. Or it might be someone on the team who wants to make a connection, to see if the candidate would fit in." Another reason for a second interview might be that the company wants to ask more in-depth questions or to provide more insight into its needs.

While second interviews are the norm, if you're asked back for a third or fourth, there are probably other factors at play. Here, hiring managers explain why you might be called back repeatedly—and what you can do to prove once and for all that you're the right person for the job.

CONFIDENCE VERSUS COCKINESS

Some candidates, in an effort to appear confident, actually overdo the role and appear egocentric instead. Susan Cheng says that she has encountered this type of interviewee. "There's a thin line between being confident and being prideful," she explains. "For example, there was one gentleman who had all the right qualifications. There was a moment in the interview when we asked, 'If you were in this position, what would be the first three things you would do?' The guy basically said, 'I would change everything.' He was trying to be very confident in his approach, but that came across the wrong way." What could this candidate have done to prevent this situation from occurring? He should have worked on his delivery, using more diplomacy and tactfulness. "Word choice is important," reminds Cheng.

On a callback interview, make sure not to overstep the boundary into arrogance. It's one thing to be sure of your abilities, but quite another to question the abilities of those around you.

CONFLICTING REPORTS

A candidate may also be called in for multiple interviews because the various interviewers can't reach a consensus. Explains Cheng: "The person might come in and interview with six people. Ideally, [the interviewers] could decide [the candidate's suitability] at that point. But if one out of six interviewers says, 'No, it's not a good fit,' it's not a majority-win situation. So [another] interview might be required to get more data points on the candidate." Another hiring manager at a global IT corporation reiterates this idea. He says, "I've seen people stumble because they might have had great interviews in the beginning, but they are now overconfident and underprepared. They might think they now have a rubberstamp of approval, but that's never the case. One interviewer could definitely veto the process, because they're already on the team and they carry a lot of weight."

There isn't necessarily an easy cure for conflicting reports, since you may never know which of your interviewers—if any—is barring your entrance into the company. The best you can do is to treat each interviewer with civility and consideration. Be yourself, be prepared, and if this isn't enough to earn a job offer, take solace in the fact you'll eventually find an employer that is a better fit.

SECOND IN LINE

Another reason you might be called back multiple times is if you were second in the line for the job, but the number one person didn't come through. A hiring manager for an accounting firm in New York City says, "In this situation, we call people back in order to evaluate them as the preferred candidate rather than a possibility."

As each interview represents a fresh beginning, it would be unwise to coast on the success of a previous interview. If you were previously second in line, you will have to prove to the interviewers that you are indeed the best of the remaining candidates. This means you will have to research and prepare not just for the first interview, but also for each subsequent callback.

A NAGGING CONCERN

A hiring manager for a market research company says that he would call back a candidate if he or another interviewer has concerns about one aspect of that candidate's qualifications. He says, "In one instance, we needed a person who had both extensive programming skills *and* market research capabilities, including experience building, testing, administering, and reviewing online surveys. We called back several candidates, but each one seemed to have either strong programming skills or strong market research skills. When we finally found someone who seemed to possess both, we were concerned that although he had some programming skills, these weren't extensive enough. And in fact, after three or four interviews, we decided against making an offer to this candidate."

If you suspect that your interviewer has a concern about you, it's best to follow the advice of David Wittenberg, a manager, and to be upfront about the situation. Ask your interviewer what concerns, if any, he has about you. That way, you can address these issues directly during the interview process, rather than speculate about them after the fact.

IN CONTENTION FOR A DIFFERENT POSITION

"Another reason [for multiple interviews] might be that the candidate was applying for one position, but we liked that person and his qualifications and thought he would fit another," says Cheng. In other words, your interviewer might prefer to place you in a position other than the one you are interviewing for. Unless your interviewer is up-front about the company's intentions, it's impossible to know if this is a reason why you might be receiving multiple callbacks. The best thing to do is to continue to tout whatever expertise you have that is directly applicable to the position requirements, while also mentioning more universal skills.

Real-Life Interview Mishaps (and What You Can Learn from Them)

Forgotten names! Rambling interviewers! Impromptu trips to the restroom! Current and former jobseekers describe their stickiest interview situations and offer tips on how to outwit them.

The Problem: A Forgotten Name

Ben O'Connell, a producer in programming operations, says his most harrowing interview situation involved a lapse of memory. "When I first interviewed for my current position, I spoke with someone from human resources, then I spoke with someone who was the director of my division," he says. "The HR person told me to go downstairs and to stand by a specific door to meet the director. I was given the director's name, but as soon as I got to the door, I realized I had forgotten it. The director introduced herself, but halfway through the interview I had forgotten her name *again*. As part of the interview, I had to take a written test. I took it, walked out of the room, which was a conference room, and tried to figure out how to approach her without knowing her name. Thankfully, she saw me coming and she took the test from me. We chatted for a couple of minutes and I left. I didn't know her name until after I had been hired and was introduced to her again for the third time."

The Solution: A Memory Trick

O'Connell says, "[I attribute this situation] to nerves and being bad with names. I've always been told that when you meet someone, to repeat their name—I tried that and I still forgot her name." While this trick failed for O'Connell, repeating a name can sometimes help to plant it more firmly in your head. Another memory trick is to associate the name with an already established idea or object, thus establishing a mental bridge between old information and new. One jobseeker offers a first-hand example of name associations. "I had an interviewer with the last name 'Piazza,'" she says. "This sounded to me like, 'pizza,' so whenever I saw the guy, I thought 'pizza' and the name would come to me automatically." For more information on remembering names, see pg. 50.

The Problem: An Interviewer Who Loves the Sound of His Own Voice

Some interviewers really grill their candidates in an attempt to extract as much information as possible. Others, however, prefer to chitchat about sports, the weather, anything but you and your potential fit within the organization. Says one job-seeker: "My interviewer blew a full twenty-five minutes on nothing. By the time [he had finished] I had only five or ten minutes left to talk, and I was so eager to get everything out that I sounded rushed."

The Solution: Being a Good Listener

If you're stuck with a loquacious interviewer, it's not necessarily in your best interest to cut him off. You run the risk of seeming rude. Besides, if your interviewer is so enamored of his own voice, he probably won't want to listen to someone else's. In this case, your best bet is to pay close attention to everything your interviewer says, especially any information pertaining to the open position. Leigh Wetzel, the online manager, agrees with this tactic. "Listening works really well," she explains. "Sometimes, the interviewer will do all the talking in an interview. And they'll come out thinking you're very intelligent if you just maintain eye contact and listen."

The Problem: An Awkward Interaction

A chatty interviewer is one problem, but what about the interviewer who asks a question and then watches in silence as you flounder? Manager Shawn Jarrett says one of his interviews was memorable for its awkwardness. "One company made me an offer—but I don't really know why. They were asking specific economic questions, and my answers didn't make sense," he says. "I couldn't even complete a sentence. I had never sweated so much in my life. I literally had to go to the bathroom to wipe off my face, and I was thinking of not even going back into the interviewing room."

The Solution: Readiness

Jarrett says, "Make sure you can weave your whole story together in a seamless way." If that fails, he also suggests giving yourself a moment to think. "Make sure you have a glass of water with you," he advises. "You need something to give you time to pause. Take a gulp of water, and you will have time to think about a difficult question. That way there won't be any deafening silences."

The Problem: A Skeptical Interviewer

One jobseeker fresh out of college became anxious when her interviewer asked her why she thought she was qualified for the position. "I had decent editorial skills," she explains. "I'd worked on both a literary magazine and a newspaper while in college. But I was applying for a job in television broadcasting. When my interviewer told me, 'I'm not sure you have the experience we're looking for,' in my heart I agreed with her."

The Solution: Absolute Confidence in Your Own Abilities

While this jobseeker might not have had ideal experience—and in fact, "ideal experience" is a rarity in the workplace—some of her skills were indeed transferable. She might have succeeded in convincing her interviewer that she was capable of performing the job if she had cited these transferable skills and given concrete examples of relevant achievements. "Never look at a job description and think you're not qualified—it's the art of the sell," says Shawn Jarrett. Indeed, the candidate who doubts herself will have the interviewer doubting her too. Continues Jarrett: "I might compare the job requirements to my skills and not see a perfect match, but I'll ask, 'Is there anything in this job description that I couldn't learn?'"

The Problem: A Job That Doesn't Pay Enough

One candidate completed an interview at a company that seemed like a great fit. The only hitch was that while the job seemed like it would be challenging and fulfilling, it didn't pay enough. "I was living in Boston," he explains. "Just to pay rent would be half my salary—maybe over half. Even if I [were] offered the job, I honestly didn't know if I could support myself on what they would be offering." This jobseeker says that he was asked back for a second interview, but turned down the chance. "I've [since] wondered if I made a mistake," he admits.

The Solution: Weighing All Your Options

Accepting a job with a salary that could leave you homeless is obviously a bad idea. However, *interviewing* for such a job is another story. Any interview experience is good interview experience, as you will learn more about the process and probably improve your communication skills along the way.

If the job you're interviewing for offers a less-than-ideal salary, as opposed to a completely unrealistic salary, don't be so quick to balk. In an unsteady job market, a lower-paying position is better than unemployment. At least you'll continue to hone your skills while keeping yourself in the workforce. And there's always the potential for a raise or even a promotion. Says one professional, Kathleen Pierce: "Especially for people who are right out of college, don't be afraid to take a job that isn't that great—or that isn't exactly what you want—because you don't know where it will lead. For [my] law firm job, I didn't like it that much, but it eventually led to an Internet job that I loved. The Internet company was a client of the law firm I was working for—I made friends with them. So you never know what will happen."

Key Chapter Points

+ "Fit" is defined by how compatible a candidate is with a specific corporate culture. Use the interview as an opportunity to consider if the company's environment corresponds with who you are and how you work. Your interviewer will be considering your fit from the employer's perspective.

+ The most common type of interview follows a one-on-one format, in which you—as the candidate—speak to one interviewer at a time. Other interview formats include the panel or committee interview, the phone interview, the group interview, the stress interview, the lunch or dinner interview, and the videoconference interview.

✦ Throughout the interview, pay attention to the cues you're sending your interviewer. These include obvious responses, such as the content of your answers, to more subtle communications like your mannerisms and speech patterns. A limp handshake or a lack of eye contact can spell disaster during an interview.

✦ While second interviews are extremely common, third or fourth interviews may signal trouble ahead. Employers may ask you back for multiple interviews if there is a lack of consensus among a panel of interviewers or if your confidence is being construed as arrogance, for instance. Be mindful of the potential reasons for multiple callbacks, and prepare for each interview with renewed vigilance and determination.

✦ The day after your interview, always mail a handwritten thank-you note to your interviewer. In the note emphasize your ability to meet the challenges of the job, thank the interviewer for her time and consideration, and reiterate your strong interest in the position.

Chapter Nine

HELP—NO ONE'S BITING!

In a tough job market, and sometimes even in a healthy, robust one, finding a job can seem like the equivalent of scaling Mount Everest with one hand tied behind your back. You can send out hundreds of résumés without a single reply. You can call dozens of hiring managers only to hear irritated responses and abrupt hang-ups. You can contact every member of your network without finding a lead. The process can leave you feeling dejected. And the worst part of it is, while interviewers are looking for confident candidates, the job search can wreak havoc on your self-esteem, leaving you insecure. One jobseeker, who has been unemployed for about six months, says, "How can I be self-assured when doors have been slamming in my face? On an interview—when I'm lucky enough to get one—I try to hide my doubts, but I'm sure they show through."

There are no easy solutions to the dismay that accompanies a difficult job search. Sometimes the best you can do is to be easy on yourself. If you're exploring all possible avenues with no success, there's no sense castigating yourself or questioning your abilities or self-worth. A job search requires diligence and effort, but there is also some alchemy in the mix. Timing and luck—things beyond your control—also play their parts. What *is* within your control is continuing your search in a healthful way—that is, in a way that doesn't leave you feeling downhearted. Below are some tips for striking the right balance.

Ways to Ride Out the Dry Spells

STICK TO YOUR SCHEDULE

One way to ride out a rocky job search is to remember that work is only that: work. It is one component of your life—an important component, to be sure—but certainly not the only one, even when your livelihood depends on it. During your job search, devoting every waking hour to looking for and applying to jobs is not a good idea. Your job search should be balanced with other activities, especially those that you enjoy. Perhaps the best way to keep the job search in perspective is to make a schedule for yourself, as discussed in chapter 1. If you're not doing so already, allot a certain period of time each day to the employment process, but leave some time for other pursuits. Then, no matter how you're feeling when you wake up each morning, stick to that schedule. It will give you an agenda so that each day doesn't become a procession of hours without parameters.

One former jobseeker, who is now employed as a senior graphic designer, says that she set a job-search-related goal for herself each day. "When I was unemployed," she says, "I attempted to apply for five jobs every day." She mostly filled out online job applications on job search sites and performed follow-up by e-mailing and phoning. She continues, "Applying for so many jobs doesn't mean you're going to be excited about half—or even more than half—of the positions. But it's important to get out there." After the graphic designer had met her daily quota, she tried to steer her thoughts away from the job search. In this way, she didn't become fixated on what can become an all-consuming process. Says another former jobseeker: "It's all too easy to sit at a computer and to browse through Monster or HotJobs for five or six hours at a clip. After awhile, your brain goes dead and when you finally get up from your chair, you're left with a feeling of 'I feel terrible—what happened to my day?'" Others find it helpful to consider job-seeking their full-time jobs. They work at the process during ordinary business hours—nine to five, for example, with a lunch break.

However much time you allot to your search, leave room for healthful activities such as meditation, prayer, sports, walking, gardening, drawing, writing, cooking, or any other activity that makes you feel good. Make time to see friends and family, too. Some people have a habit of isolating themselves through periods of unemployment—yet seeing people is important, because unemployment can breed loneliness. Spending time with people you like will buoy your spirits. It will also, incidentally, reinforce your personal and professional network.

CONTINUE TO FOLLOW UP

Chapter 6 underscored the importance of following up, including calling or e-mailing every hiring manager to make sure they received your résumé and cover letter. Yet if you've applied for scores of jobs, there's a chance you didn't contact every single employer to reiterate your interest in the position and to see if it is still open. Hopefully, you've used your Potential Employer List to keep a record of the jobs you applied for, the dates you applied, the names and contact information of the hiring managers, etc. Now is a good time to update that list. Go through each and every position. Have you tried to contact each company a maximum of three times? What was each company's response? Were there certain companies that seemed more receptive than others? Have you asked for informational interviews at those companies that seemed receptive?

Now is good time to update your network, too. Perhaps weeks or even months have passed since you last spoke with certain contacts. Perhaps new opportunities have arisen in that time. Go ahead and call, e-mail, or visit those people you haven't touched base with in a while. You don't have to spend much—or even any—money in the process. You can ask members of your network over for coffee, for instance, or meet in a nearby park for a brown bag lunch.

In catching up with your contacts, reiterate your job situation and ask again if they know of any possible openings. The working world can lead to feast as surely as it can lead to famine. You can go months without a single lead, but if you continue to network, you may eventually find multiple opportunities arising suddenly and simultaneously. Such was the case for Jordan Montminy, now a freelance film and TV editor. "The longest time [I went without employment] was two to three months. I made calls to the people I had worked with previously and inquired whether they needed help. This was also at a time when I wasn't completely established as an editor yet. In a lot of people's minds, I was still in the editor assistant phase, [so] I had some convincing to do. I finally received a call out of the blue from a company I'd worked with before—they needed someone to take the graveyard shift. The job came at the right time. And shortly after that, I ended up getting another call from a friend I'd worked with on a previous show, and in the course of the conversation she casually mentioned that she was looking for an editor. Of course I eagerly offered my services."

LEARN FROM YOUR MISTAKES

Often, you can benefit from seemingly futile efforts. If you've had an interview but were never given an offer, ask your interviewer if there was anything you could have improved upon. Many interviewers will be happy to tell you the reason or reasons why you were passed over. There's no harm in asking; in fact, you can only gain by listening to your interviewer's insights. If you can correct a problem or improve a weak spot, you will be more prepared for subsequent interview opportunities, as reported by one jobseeker who took the initiative: "My interviewer called to tell me that they'd picked someone else for the position. I was really disappointed, but I asked him if he could give me any advice on my performance. He gave me one or two suggestions, which were helpful. I think I earned his respect by asking. Even though he didn't pick me for the job, I think he saw that I'm someone who is always striving to be better."

STAY HOPEFUL

Bill Waldorf, an MBA and licensed counselor with a certification in career counseling, says, "People's careers are tied to their self identity, their livelihood, social support, lifestyle, friends, day-to-day routine, self-respect, social identity, sense of belonging, and so much more. . . . Is it any wonder why careers affect people so much?" No, it's no wonder at all. Careers do have tremendous meaning, especially in a society where people are constantly asking, "So, what is it that you do?"

If you're unemployed, you may feel worried and alone—as if part of your identity has been damaged or is missing. While maintaining a healthy lifestyle will help you to keep your head above water during this difficult period, so too will sheer optimism. Bear in mind that you *will* find a job eventually, if not necessarily today or tomorrow. The knowledge that things are bound to improve can be a great source of comfort if you're out of work for an extended period of time. In fact, hope and faith are perhaps the best elixirs for the unemployment blues.

Like so many professionals, Ben O'Connell endured many rejections before a golden opportunity came his way. "Right after college... I looked at every publisher in the San Francisco Bay Area and sent them all letters," he says. "I received responses from maybe 10 percent of the total. Most responses were 'We'll keep your résumé on file'—in other words, 'Thanks, but no thanks.' One letter, in particular, came from a small publishing company that specializes in minority and women's histories and local histories. The president of the company wrote a personal letter saying how much he liked my résumé and experience, but at this time they didn't have anything available. I thought this was another example of 'Thanks, but no thanks,' but about four months later, the president himself called me out of blue to say that he had a number of possibilities open now. I went in to interview—and it went extraordinarily well." O'Connell's situation is just one example of how one's employment prospects are bound to improve eventually.

Additional Strategies

GO BACK TO THE BASICS

Another way to outwit unemployment is to go back to the basics. Start with your Personal Career Inventory, which you worked on in chapter 1. In the inventory, you considered what you have to offer an employer; you also thought about what you want in one. Now go back and see if the job search has changed your perspective. Perhaps at the time that you started your job search you believed you wanted to work in a certain field, or you didn't want to accept any job below a certain salary range, or you didn't want to commute more than a specified distance. If you've met with a lot of adversity in your search for the right job, you may want to rethink your strategy. By broadening your criteria you may usher in more opportunities.

Tweaking the parameters of your Personal Career Inventory doesn't mean you're selling out or giving up your dreams. It means only that you're willing to adjust in light of difficult circumstances. Especially if you are a recent graduate, or if the economy is tumultuous, there's nothing shameful about making certain sacrifices for the sake of reentering the workforce. In fact, employers see the ability to adapt as a plus. Says one recruiter: "Don't be scared about paying your dues, especially early in your career. You're going to enhance your experience. And you're going to get the tools you need to climb the ladder later on."

In addition to reevaluating your Personal Career Inventory, you may want to revisit the section in chapter 1 entitled "Help—I Don't Know My Future Career Plans!" Contained in this section are several ideas that might be of help not only to the uncertain jobseeker, but also to the jobseeker who *does* know her future career plans. For instance, by becoming a temp you can ease the financial burden of being unemployed. If you are struggling to enter the industry of your choice, becoming a temporary staff member in that industry may eventually lead to a full-time offer or to important employment connections. When there is no other "in," temping can provide that elusive gateway, especially if you can temp for a company on your Prospective Employer List.

Taking a class in your prospective sector—an idea also introduced in "Help—I Don't Know My Future Career Plans!"—is another way to inject new life into your job search. Is there a weak spot on your résumé? Is there a skill that needs enhancing? Have any potential employers told you that they wish you had a little bit more know-how in a certain area? If so, taking a class might help you to become more well-rounded, thus making you more attractive to employers.

BECOME AN INTERN OR VOLUNTEER

If you're eager to work but haven't received an offer yet, consider becoming an intern. As with temping, interning may lead to fresh leads, and if you're lucky, an offer of permanent employment. Moreover, companies are often more likely to hire interns than full-time employees because they don't have to invest as much in salaries, health care insurance, etc. Companies generally don't pay interns very much money, and some interns opt to work for free simply to gain experience and exposure. If you're strapped for cash and can't picture yourself interning on a full-time basis, consider becoming a part-time intern at a company that truly interests you. Any internship experience—as long as it's meaningful—may help you in the long run.

Melissa Walker, an associate editor, calls her previous internships "invaluable," for it helped her to get started in the business. She says, "My first interview ever was for [an internship] at a women's magazine. I came down from college and I was very nervous. But later in the summer after the internship was nearly over, my editor was speaking at an intern lunch, and she said, 'I want to tell you about Melissa Walker and why she got hired.' She'd asked me on my interview, 'How devoted will you be to this job?' And I'd said, 'This job would be my whole summer, the only reason I'd be in New York.' That cinched it for her."

Like an internship, meaningful volunteer work may persuade a hesitant employer to give you a chance. When scouting out volunteer work opportunities, keep your industry in mind. Try to be a volunteer in an organization within your desired field, or to do volunteer work that requires skills that you wish to use once you're employed. That way, you'll be able to add your volunteer work to your résumé, thus filling in the gap between your last job and your future job.

While interning or volunteering might not seem like ideal solutions to unemployment, either is a legitimate short-term band-aid. Recruiters and employers across the board say that when it comes to outwitting the job market, doing something is better than doing nothing.

REACH OUT TO A MENTOR

In the workplace a mentor is a trusted adviser, someone who will guide you as you strive to make the most of your career. Some employers have an official mentoring system, pairing a more seasoned worker with someone who is new to the company. Some companies also have official mentoring programs for women or members of minority groups. Many clubs, trade organizations, and associations also foster mentorship programs for their members.

Nevertheless, the vast majority of mentoring is done on a more informal basis. Often, two professionals will become friends and establish a close connection. The more experienced professional may casually offer advice and counsel to the other. Such a mentoring situation can occur naturally—perhaps the two people once worked in the same department or collaborated on a project together. A mentoring situation may also evolve by way of request. David Wittenberg, a manager, says, "In my company, one of our three major growth initiatives is talent development. So, that makes it quite easy for me to pick up the phone and call a senior executive and say, 'In the spirit of our corporate initiative to develop talent, could you spare twenty-five minutes to discuss career development in our company, or career development in your department, or even your personal career development?' I've used this technique quite successfully."

You don't necessarily need to be employed to have a mentor, either. Think of professionals you worked with at previous jobs and reach out to them; or, use your college alumni network, discussed in chapter 3, to contact more seasoned professionals in your industry.

Shawn Jarrett is another strong believer in the power of mentors. Yet one of his experiences indicates that a mentor will not necessarily take a kind and gentle approach to a "mentee." Some mentors prefer brutal honesty, knowing that this candor will illuminate a person's weaknesses and help him to improve. Jarrett speaks about one mentor who used this approach with much success. "I interviewed with EDS (Electronic Data Systems)," he says. "I still remember the name of this guy, my interviewer, even to this day. I sat down to talk to this guy, and he picked me apart. He was a real HR guy—not a fly-by-night amateur. He said, 'You're not ready for our MBA training program. Let me tell you why you're not ready. You have no work experience, one. Two, you have a lot of skills but your problem is that these skills are still raw. Maybe in five to seven years you'll be ready for this program.' He interviewed me twice—once in the fall and once in the spring, to see if I'd gotten any better. He made me an offer as a direct hire, rather than as an MBA initiate, so he saw something in me. In retrospect, he was right about what he said. . . . The moral of the story is sometimes you run into the real deal, and if they give you advice, I suggest you take it."

CONSIDER FREELANCING

In a rough economy, working for yourself—as opposed to a company—is an option for some. Freelancing can allow you to work for several different employers, or clients, without being tied down to only one. It can also enable to make your own hours, set your own pace, and work from the convenience of your home or personal office. At the same time, freelancing is no joyride. Freelancers have to look for new clients on a constant basis, as each project has a limited duration and there is no guarantee that more projects will come down the same pipelines. In addition, freelancers have to set their own rates, make sure clients pay on time, purchase their own health insurance (sometimes at higher, non-group premiums), and network as if it were going out of style, among other tasks.

Yet those who freelance swear that the perks are sizable. "One of the many advantages of being a freelancer is that your jobs are not permanent so you are used to looking for work constantly," says Jordan Montminy, a freelance film and TV editor. "If you do have a stretch when you're not working, you're used to it—it comes with the territory. You are not going to be as panicked, compared to someone who has been working for the same company for fifteen years and has been laid off." Melissa Walker agrees that freelancing can be a good option. Although Walker has since opted for a full-time position with a company, she talks about her successful stint as a freelance journalist and how she was guided by a mentor. "My first executive editor at the magazine where I worked has definitely been a huge influence on me," she says. "When we all got laid off, I sent out my résumé like crazy, but she said, 'Look, you'll get another job. I'll hire you.' She was the one who steered me toward freelancing. I'd only written four or five freelance articles at that point and I had only a few contacts. But she said, 'You can do it. You can set up a home office. You have the discipline.' She said that I shouldn't take a job I wouldn't really like just because I felt jobless. She made me more confident about my career. I would have been too scared otherwise and taken any job that came along."

Walker touches upon an attribute that is a must-have for any freelancer: discipline. Those who like structure, lots of interaction with other people, and conventional office life will probably not function well working on their own. Freelancing requires a tremendous amount of self-motivation and self-reliance. Freelancers must be both managers and employees—tackling each new project with authority and efficiency. Even one lax, unproductive day can upset their schedules, leading to setbacks, stress, and disgruntled clients.

If you have self-motivation in spades, and think freelancing might suit your lifestyle and work style, talk to other freelancers before you start. Learn how others have made their way and what obstacles they've had to overcome. You'll be better off learning from the mistakes of others than making your own. Also, make sure your industry is freelancer-friendly. While freelancers exist in all industries, some fields are easier to break into than others. It helps if you've already been in your sector for a number of years and have ready-made contacts and clients to rely on—at least at first. You may be able to find work on freelance job sites, too. Popular sites include Guru (www.guru.com), Elance (www.elance.com), and Sologig (www.sologig.com). Also, check out the National Association for the Self-Employed (www.nase.org), which is a solid information resource.

If you're currently unemployed and stuck in a sluggish job market, exploring freelancing as an option might be worth your while. Says Walker: "Freelancing is a plus and a minus in [a bad] economy. Employers don't want to hire anyone full-time, but they do need people, so freelancers become more popular." Montminy, who has worked as a freelancer for several years, sees the silver lining even more clearly. "In these troubled times," he declares, "I think being a freelancer gives a person some peace of mind." To be sure, there's no need to worry about pink slips, pay caps, or the sudden loss of health insurance and other benefits. If you choose freelancing, you'll be the master of your own fate.

Key Chapter Points

+ Don't be too hard on yourself if your job search is taking longer than you expected or if it is not yielding as many leads as you would have hoped. Sticking to a daily schedule that includes time for your job search as well as time for healthful and enjoyable activities will help to lift your spirits.

✦ Continue to update your Prospective Employer List by following up on every position for which you applied and recording your findings. Update your network, too, by communicating with people you haven't been in touch with for a while. New employment opportunities may have arisen in the interim.

✦ Ask past interviewers to give you feedback on what you could have done better in your interviews. Some interviewers will be willing to tell you the reason or reasons why you didn't progress in the hiring process. Use this information to correct any problems or to strengthen any weak spots, thereby improving your odds in future interviews.

✦ Finding a mentor, freelancing, or becoming an intern or volunteer within your desired industry are all good strategies for surviving a stint of unemployment and forging new paths into the workplace.

Chapter Ten

WAHOOO—A JOB OFFER! NOW WHAT?

Evaluating Your Offer: Factors to Consider Once an Offer Is on the Table

A job offer has come in. Elation and relief flood through you. Those long weeks or months of perseverance have finally paid off. There's a good chance you won't have to pore over any more job advertisements for a good long time. But the process isn't over yet. To close the deal you'll have to take some final steps. These include negotiating your salary and benefits and submitting a job offer acceptance letter to the company. Of course, the first thing to consider is whether you want the job at all.

If you've been job-hunting for a long time, it's tempting take the first job that's offered. Sometimes this is the wisest thing to do. After all, as the old adage goes, a bird in the hand is worth two in the bush. Yet if you have skills that are in high demand, are working in a rapidly growing sector, are waiting for confirmation on another pending offer, or are simply hesitant about working for the company in question, you'll want to evaluate the offer very carefully. Remember that if you commit to a job, you're likely to be there for a minimum of twelve months or else risk being labeled a job-hopper. And while one year may not seem like a long time, even one day at the office can seem like an eternity if you don't like your job. Thus, even if you're eager to confirm your acceptance of the offer, take a little time—even twenty-four hours—to be absolutely sure that the position is right for you.

What is the right way to go about evaluating a job offer? Once again, your Personal Career Inventory may come in handy. Take a long, hard look at your vital employment information, especially in Steps Two and Three where you considered what you wanted and didn't want in a position, and then funneled down this information to a few key points. Now compare the job you are being offered against those key points. There is no such thing as a perfect job—one that will meet every single one of your needs. But some jobs are certainly better than others. Does the job in question meet *most* of the criteria you listed on your Personal Career Inventory? Are the concessions that you will have to make minimal, or at very least, tolerable? You are the only person who can decide.

If you're currently employed, does the job on the table surpass the quality of your present job in terms of the criteria you listed? Sometimes the best way to decide is to evaluate the jobs side by side. Tabulate the "pros" and "cons" of each of the positions, then see which of the two comes out ahead. The same strategy goes if you're in the lucky predicament of evaluating two separate job offers. Use your Personal Career Inventory as the basis for deciding which of the offers has more of the pros that are most important to you and fewer of the cons. Don't forget that some of the pros, such as a high base salary or great benefits, may be more important than others—so give more weight to those criteria that you consider essential.

Using your Personal Career Inventory will help you to evaluate an offer with logic, clarity, and objectivity. Yet you shouldn't ignore your emotions in the process. If you are strongly drawn to a position for reasons that are not instantly quantifiable, don't ignore your gut instinct. It should be strongly factored into your decision-making process.

Money in Hand: How to Negotiate Your Compensation

If you've finished evaluating the job offer and have decided that the position is indeed right for you, the next step is to speak to the company about compensation and benefits.

First and foremost, keep in mind that negotiating compensation is simply not possible for every jobseeker. If you've been hired for an entry-level position or are fresh out of school with little work experience, you may not have the bargaining power you need to negotiate. An HR manager at a federal judiciary underscores this point when speaking about the hiring process where he works. "We have a lot more flexibility in our system because it's a decentralized system. [But] if we're hiring a bunch of newbies, there isn't much discussion. We are going to tell them that since they are entry-level and since there are rapid raises built into the system—in two years their income will go up about 25 percent—they'll start at the bottom," he says. Some jobs, especially those associated with government agencies or unions, have salary caps that are strictly enforced. No matter how persuasive or charming you might be, in this case salary negotiation is probably not an option. In a bear market, too, salary negotiation is less likely to occur. Explains an HR manager at an international IT provider: "These days there has been no negotiation. [Candidates] have just taken our offers. But I think it's still good to negotiate—even in this tough market. Just don't push it too hard." Indeed, if you push too hard for higher compensation, your employer may regard you as ungrateful, aggressive, or demanding. You may alienate people at your company before you even begin your job.

In the scenarios above, salary negotiation is a questionable endeavor. Yet in most other cases, most jobseekers can and should negotiate. Melissa Walker, who works in the magazine industry, says, "People don't realize that they can negotiate, especially if it's not an entry-level job. The salary they offer you isn't what they can give you; it's what they want you to take." Walker is absolutely right. Companies seldom approach negotiation with only one number in mind. They can be flexible if candidates can positively and persuasively argue why they deserve more.

By the same token, companies don't decide compensation in an erratic fashion. Most employers have in place a compensation determination process based on factors like a candidate's skills, experience, and previous income. The state of the economy, a company's budget allocations, and internal salary structures may also come into play. A senior human resources consultant at an insurance company explains how compensation is determined at her company. "We're not shy about the salary issue here," she says. "We talk to our candidates about salary during our phone screens—I bring it up; I don't like it when they do. I explain the company philosophy regarding compensation. During the face-to-face interview, candidates are given forms where they explain their salary matters completely. The way we structure our offers is based on market information, so our offers are really well thought out and fair. We do not negotiate at all." While most companies *are* open to negotiation, at least to some extent, it's important to know up front if your company is not. In all likelihood, you'll find this out through your research—if a company representative doesn't inform you first.

EDUCATE YOURSELF

As with every stage of outwitting the job market, compensation negotiation comes down to preparation. Before you speak with the company representative regarding compensation, do your homework. Find out what the salary range is for the type of job you are being offered, keeping in mind that your level of experience should be factored into the equation and that salaries vary greatly by region. (Thirty thousand dollars goes a lot farther in New Holstein, Wisconsin, than it does in San Francisco, California, for example). Before you approach negotiations, you'll want to have a salary range in your head, including the lowest base salary you would be willing to accept through to a more enticing sum. Anything above your range would be, of course, icing on the cake.

You can figure out a practical range by researching salary survey sites like Salary (www.salary.com) and SalaryExpert (www.salaryexpert.com). On these sites you will be asked to enter information about your industry, job title, and/or geographic region. When you're finished, the sites will approximate the anticipated range of your base salary. Another helpful site is WageWeb (www.wageweb.com), which offers national wage averages in industries such as Finance, Engineering, Health Care, Manufacturing, and Human Resources. JobStar (www.jobstar.org) is another first-rate site for salary survey information.

Be sure to cross-check the information on these sites with other sources, especially those compiled by government or employment agencies. The Wages, Earnings & Benefits Web page on the Department of Labor's Website (www.dol.gov/dol/topic/statistics/wagesearnings.htm) is a helpful resource. Here, compensation information is categorized by geographic region, occupation, and industry. The site also has, in some cases, "additional categories, such as age, sex, or union membership." If, in accepting a position, you would be moving from one city to another, or even from one state to another, you'll want to know how much you would have to earn to maintain your standard of living. The "Salary Calculator" on Homefair (www.homefair.com/homefair/calc/salcalc.html?type=to) will tell you how much more or less you would have to make in order to keep up with your regular expenses.

Of course, the best way to determine an acceptable salary range is by talking to knowledgeable employees in your industry, especially those employees who hold jobs similar to the one you are considering. Before taking any new job, Eric Thompson, a programmer, makes it a point to ask around about compensation. "I would always talk to people in the same industry, the same sector, and find out what they were making," he says. "In all my jobs I've found wild disparities among people in similar positions at the same company. I was at a company where I was told by management not to tell others what I was making. But

one night three or four of us coworkers were out to dinner and we decided to tell each other our salaries. It turned out that those of us who
shared information were making similar amounts. But we found out
we were making five to fifty thousand dollars less than other coworkers with similar job titles." While many employees may be open to
speaking with you about compensation, others will be more guarded.
In some cases, people are simply uncomfortable speaking about what
they regard as a private issue. In other cases, as Thompson's experience attests, employees are bound by company policy to nondisclosure
regarding compensation.

While speaking with others in your industry about compensation
is worthwhile, you should also keep your own circumstances in mind. If
this is your first job, if you are entering a new industry with little related experience, if you are working in a sector that doesn't pay much,
or if you are living in a tony locale, you'll also need to think about your
personal budget and how much money you'll have to earn in order to
cover your monthly expenses such as rent or mortgage payments, commuting costs, utilities, groceries, etc. Your lowest acceptable salary
should be a livable wage—that is, it should cover your bare necessities,
at the very least. Don't underestimate what your lowest acceptable
salary should be, as you'll regret it later, each time your bank account
runs dry before the end of the month.

Many jobseekers, whether or not they are new to the job market,
make the mistake of approaching negotiation with base numbers that
are too low. They worry that their desired salaries are too high, but they
overcompensate for this worry by deflating their expectations. One professional who works for the online business of a consumer goods company negotiated her salary, but has one regret. "If I would have done
things differently," she says, "I would have asked for an additional ten
thousand rather than five thousand because they might have come back
and said, 'We can't give you ten but we'll throw you a bone and give
you five.' If you start with five, the upside is [not as great]." A professional who works in the Washington, D.C. area says that he didn't even

attempt to negotiate his salary, thereby eliminating his chances for greater compensation. "I wish I had [negotiated my salary]," he reveals. "I would have placed a higher desired salary on the application, and after being offered the job, I probably would have asked for five thousand dollars more."

CONSIDER ALL ELEMENTS OF THE PACKAGE

Negotiation mostly revolves around salaries, but issues like bonuses, flex-time, relocation assistance, and tuition reimbursement may also end up on the bargaining table. It all depends on what is important to you and your lifestyle, and of course, what the company is willing to negotiate. In your Personal Career Inventory you have already prioritized which issues are of utmost importance to you. As you approach negotiation, keep your eye on the overall package, rather than simply the number you want to see on your paycheck.

Beth Camp, the owner of a professional placement service, stresses that salary is not the only thing on the minds of most candidates. "It may not be simply base salary that will close the deal," she explains. "Most times, actually, it's not. Many times an assurance of flexibility for daycare, observance of uncommon religious holidays, specific vacation issues, or off-cycle review/raise alternatives will offset a monetary difference and convince an applicant to take the job. Sometimes something as simple as providing reimbursement for an extra-long commute or city work taxes will be the deciding factor."

Once you finalize what compensation terms are important to you and your lifestyle, commit them to memory. When you approach negotiations, you'll want to know these items inside and out. Susan Cheng, a manager at a media entertainment company, offers good advice on how a candidate should present these requests when meeting with the company representative. "One thing an individual should do is to lay out all negotiable items, not just salary. Make sure you know what's most important to you. Ask for a few items at a time. If the answer comes back

'No' from your employer, you can request the second set. Understand what your negotiable items are, but don't lay them out all at once. You'll have a better likelihood of the employer agreeing to something if you lay them out in stages."

In an unstable economy, more and more candidates are keeping in mind that no job lasts forever. They are taking the once unusual step of negotiating severance packages before their jobs even start. This isn't a bad idea, considering a survey and report entitled "The Disposable Worker: Living in a Job-Loss Economy," a joint project between the John J. Heldrich Center for Workforce Development at Rutgers University and the Center for Survey Research and Analysis at the University of Connecticut. According to "The Disposable Worker," 18 percent of American workers "report they were laid off from a full- or part-time job during the 2000-2003 recession." Moreover, 65 percent of those workers "were not offered a severance package or other compensation by their employer." Negotiating a severance package is not a good idea for everyone, but the fact that severance packages can be negotiated in the first place shows that candidates have quite a bit of control over what can be accomplished during the negotiation process.

IT'S ALL IN YOUR ATTITUDE

Negotiating compensation is a bit of a balancing act, for you must be persuasive and self-assured without ever seeming antagonistic or entitled. Many experts stress that the tone you project is everything. If you sound overconfident, your arguments won't matter much, even if they are cogent. "Tone in salary negotiation is important," states one human resources manager. "It's an attitude thing. Say we're willing to pay $70,000 to someone with five or ten years of experience. They could say, 'I'm not willing to consider this job for a dollar less than $70,000.' That is *not* preferable to 'I'm at $68,000 now and I would really like $70,000. If you offered me $68,000, would I take it? Yes, because the desirability of the job is high. But I would prefer $70,000.'" Thus, as this

HR manager illustrates, how you make your point is as important—if not more important—than the point itself.

Those who have little negotiation experience are particularly in danger of overstepping their limits. A human resources manager at an international IT provider encountered one such person. "There was a new college hire who pressed the salary point too hard. I didn't hear any concerns from the management team, but pushiness can make a bad impression. In salary negotiation, if someone says 'No' and then turns away, that's not someone we'd want in the organization. We want someone who can diplomatically enter into negotiation."

Perhaps the best way to gear up for negotiation is to practice, much the same way you practiced for your interviews. Ask a friend who is familiar with compensation negotiation to play the part of the company representative. When the two of you sit down to discuss what you'd like to earn on the job, videotape—or at least audiotape—the encounter. Try different techniques of negotiation, and different ways of phrasing the same concepts. After you've finished, replay the encounter and see which of your arguments were the most and least effective, and if you struck the right balance between confidence and tactfulness. If you think you can do better, try the mock negotiation again—and ask your friend to respond to your requests in different ways. You'll want to be ready for any curveballs the actual company representative throws.

Anyone can benefit from rehearsing for compensation negotiation, but women, who on average earn substantially less than men, can perhaps benefit the most. According to Linda Babcock and Sara Laschever's book, *Women Don't Ask: Negotiation and the Gender Divide,* published by the Princeton University Press, women's earnings relative to men's continue to languish at around 73 percent. Moreover, men are four times more likely than women to negotiate a first salary, which is the start of the earnings discrepancy between the genders. While many factors play a part in the wage gap, women can certainly do their part to narrow it by making a point of negotiating compensation not only in their first jobs, but also in the subsequent jobs they hold.

BE READY TO EXPLAIN WHY YOU WANT A CERTAIN NUMBER

When prepping for salary negotiations, it's not enough to know what you want. You must also be able to explain convincingly why you deserve it. In advance of negotiations day, compile a list of viable reasons why you should receive your desired salary and/or the other desired elements of your compensation package. This means avoiding self-serving comments like "I need to buy a new stereo system," and focusing instead on more grounded, credible, and carefully worded arguments that highlight what you will be contributing to your new employer and what salaries you have received in the past. "I've used past earnings as a starting point [for negotiation]," says one professional at a prestigious human resources consulting firm. "But I also consider other things—location, the culture, the kind of work a particular office is doing in comparison to what I've done in the past."

Consider, too, what special skills, knowledge, education, training, and experience you will bring to the position. Be able to back up your case with real-life examples of your value. For instance, if you have the ability to bring in new clients, tell your new employer which clients you've brought in at your previous places of employment, and how much money your past employers saved or earned as a result of the relationships you created. If you have two or three examples to bolster each of your statements, the company representative will have a better sense of what you're capable of delivering. The bottom line is that you need to convince your employer that you're worth what you're asking for. Says one HR manager in Minnesota: "We have to consider the position. Is it so critical that we have to pay top dollar? Sometimes we're willing to pay extra for certain skills."

Remember, too, that negotiating entails cooperation—and sometimes, compromise—on both sides. You should be definite about your needs, but open to different ideas in terms of how these needs are met. You may not win on every issue, so be willing to cede on those compensation requests that are less important than others.

THE SALARY DANCE—'ROUND AND 'ROUND WE GO

One hiring manager called compensation negotiation a bit like a dance—when one party takes a step, so too must the other. Yet neither side wants to be the first to move. "As an employer, I want the candidate to throw out the first number," says a human resources manager at a global technology provider. "But as a jobseeker, you want the employer to throw out the first number." Indeed, that "first number" establishes the terms for the whole negotiation process. Seldom will the subsequent numbers discussed veer far from the initial figure. For this reason, as the candidate, you want the employer to be the first to announce a number, or at the least, a range. If you're the first, you run two risks—either stating a number that is too low and shooting yourself in the foot, or else stating a number that is outside the boundaries of what the company is willing to pay you.

If for some reason the employer really pushes you to speak first, and you feel the need to oblige, cite your salary range rather than just one number. At the very least, you'll be giving yourself some latitude for further negotiation. Nevertheless, once the range is on the table, the employer will be keen to focus on the low end. It bears repeating that before you approach negotiations, you should be comfortable with what the low end is. Remember that if you don't ask for more, you'll probably never receive it.

Once the range is on the table, the salary dance picks up speed. It's possible that you and your employer will agree quickly on a base salary. It's more likely, however, that you and the company representative will continue to bargain, going back and forth, until you reach a consensus. As you discuss the issue, continue to refer to your skills and achievements, and to qualify your references with concrete examples. While you don't want to sound pompous or boastful, you do want the employer to be aware of your value. A senior graphic designer, who successfully negotiated her salary, says, "Even if you're really in love with a job, you have to give the illusion that you can always get something better if you wanted to."

At the same time, listen to what the employer has to say and be willing to acquiesce if an offer sounds equitable. After all, the best negotiations end with both parties feeling satisfied.

IF USING A CONTACT, PROCEED WITH CAUTION

If you networked with an employee at the company prior to being offered the job, it may be tempting to use this person as leverage during the compensation negotiation process. Perhaps the person ranks highly on the chain of command and has the authority to influence other employees in the company. Perhaps the person can sway even the human resources department. It may be in your best interest to enlist your contact's help during salary negotiations. But if you do, be both discreet and cautious. Hiring experts warn that using unorthodox strategies during negotiations can adversely influence how your coworkers perceive you. Says manager Susan Cheng: "Understand the channels of negotiation and respect them. Even if you know the decision-maker, don't cut a path across the other channels such as HR." Indeed, by bending the rules in your own favor, you risk annoying another employee—or even a whole department.

BE GRACIOUS, NO MATTER WHAT THE OUTCOME

Overall, "only 6 percent of both HR professionals and jobseekers indicate a frequency of nonacceptance due to unsuccessful negotiations," according to a recent poll by the Society for Human Resources Management entitled "Negotiating Rewards." The vast majority of jobseekers *are* able to successfully negotiate their compensation.

But what about the minority? If your employer comes back with an offer that is below your anticipated salary range, you do have alternatives. Says one human resources manager: "It's a perfectly fair question to ask the company, 'Can you tell me exactly why you arrived at that offer?'" It's also fair to ask what is and what is not negotiable. For example, if your employer says that your undersized base salary cannot be increased, there is always the possibility of bolstering your overall compensation package. Ask about bonuses, extra time off, an earlier compensation review date, or whatever else you think might counterbalance the lower-than-expected pay. Lastly, consider that your employer might be playing hardball—attempting to hire you for as little money as possible. If you continue to plead your case tactfully, buttressing examples of your worth with evidence of prior accomplishments, there's a chance the employer will eventually yield to your requests.

Of course, there's also a chance the employer won't budge. If the offered salary is so low that you consider it unacceptable, declining the position might be the right course of action. Just be sure not to sever any ties in the process. The appropriate way to end things is to emphasize the positive aspects of the experience, not the fact that you and the company didn't see eye to eye. You might say, for example, "I appreciate the offer, but after thinking it over, I'm afraid I can't accept it. Thank you for considering me. Perhaps in the future there will be other opportunities for us to work together. As you know, I think a great deal of your company."

A human resources manager at a federal judiciary explains that just because a candidate refuses one job offer at a company doesn't mean that person is out of the running for others. He says, "We've gone back to people we didn't hire for one job because it didn't pay enough, and said, 'Hey, we have something now.' It happens more than you might think, so don't burn your bridges."

One Professional's Compensation Negotiation Success Story

An advertising associate in New York City explains how she outwitted the compensation negotiation process by being flexible and having confidence in her own market value:

"For my present position as an advertising associate, an ads manager called me and asked if I wanted to come in for an interview. [I had been working as a freelancer and] they already had my résumé and some clips I'd sent out. I came in and met with some staff members. Later, they called me back and told me I should talk to HR. At that point, I filled out the official employment forms, but it sort of caused trouble because that was the first time I'd addressed the issue of salary—what I was making freelancing, which was actually more than my previous salary. I found out that they were offering a lot less than I'd thought.

"I told them that I couldn't take the job for such a low salary. A few days later the Director of Advertising called me and offered me more money. I would have taken [that second] offer, to be honest. But I told them I wanted to mull it over for a day. Right away he made an even higher offer. But I said I *still* wanted to think things over. At that point I knew they were flexible. I was really nervous, but I decided I wanted to try for an even higher salary that wasn't unrealistic, but that was fair and in the market range. I called him back on Monday, and said, 'If you can't meet the salary I'd like, I'm willing to listen to other ideas, like a signing bonus. I'm flexible with how I'll be compensated.' The director said, 'I don't think we can do that for you. It may be out of our range.' But he called back HR and agreed to a higher number, after all.

"I knew that no matter what happened, I had the security of [freelancing], so that was important. I don't think I would have been as bold if I were on unemployment, but I had the upper hand because I knew I could have walked away."

SALARY NEGOTIATION AND THE RECRUITER'S ROLE

Ever wonder about a recruiter's role in the salary and benefits negotiation process? Beth Camp, the owner of Two Roads Placement Service, answers a host of questions on the topic.

Q: *What is the position of the recruiter when it comes to salary and benefits negotiation with a company?*

A: The recruiter is in a unique position. He or she is the only person who always knows exactly what the applicant currently makes and wants, as well as the range the company wants to pay and how much leeway it is willing to extend to get the person it truly wants. During the interview process both parties regularly change their stances on these issues. Candidates may receive other offers. Clients may find other candidates they desire just as much with different salary requirements. It is a fluid situation.

  The recruiter manages expectations on both sides and continues educating both parties about what is . . . acceptable. If one side or the other directly throws out arbitrary numbers during interviews, [this] can completely derail the recruiter's strategy for bringing both parties together . . . or give one side an advantage. In my experience, that advantage *always* goes to the company.

Q: *Once a company extends a job offer to a candidate who is working with a recruiter, should the candidate actively participate in the salary negotiation process?*

A: The recruiter usually does all the negotiating with the client company. [Candidates] should *not* discuss salary during interviews at all. In my experience, every time candidates break that rule, they end up with a less satisfying offer or blow their shot at the job.

Q: *What, then, is the candidate's involvement?*

A: The candidate should tell the recruiter real figures and the full
compensation package at the current position. [There should be]
no surprises. The recruiter should draw out all the details, including any and all perks that a candidate currently receives. . . . Companies offer compensation packages made up of widely varying
components. Offers are accepted based on all those things. If an
applicant lies or omits any [vital information], it can become a deal
breaker in the end.

Q: *How do you deal with a candidate who has a false impression of the
salary he or she is worth?*

A: From the first, you correct that impression. If a recruiter has experience, he or she will be able to tell candidates their market values
within five to ten thousand dollars. When a good recruiter tells
you that you are over- or undervalued, listen. . . . There are always
exceptions for desperate companies that will pay anything to fill a
priority spot, but again, that will be known by the recruiter and fig-
ured into the equation. In almost all cases, the recruiter will look at
your current package and be able to tell you truthfully what you
are really worth on the market.

Q: *What, in addition to salary, do candidates want to negotiate?*

A: Training opportunities. Opportunities to improve skill sets and
expand expertise and experience. Educational reimbursement.
[Stock] options. Bonuses. Reviews and raise timetables and guarantees. Vacation. Retirement, 401(k). Religious observance flexibility. Flex-time. Medical packages. Daycare. Hours. You name
it. Everyone has a different hot button that seals the deal. Every
company has items on which they can bend and other rules set
in stone.

Q: *In your opinion, in a tough job market does salary negotiation occur less frequently?*

A: It depends. In the general population, yes. For standard positions there is such a supply of candidates that companies can adopt a "take it or leave it" stance. If one person turns the job down, another will be there to take [his or her] place. Many people who have been out of work for a long period will take anything offered, so there has been a tremendous downward pressure on salary levels. [In a given field] large percentages [of people] are taking anywhere from a five to a fifty thousand dollar cut in salary. In industries where bonuses comprise up to 50 percent of [a person's] salary, the cuts can be very extreme.

For positions that recruiters see—mainly [positions] that companies find very hard to fill on their own even in a rough economy—that pressure is less, and more negotiating occurs. If a company desperately needs a position filled, [and if it] is looking for a very specialized or scarce resource, it will be much more flexible in negotiation. It may not be extravagant in an offer, but it will work with a recruiter to tailor a package to get that applicant to accept. . . . If a recruiter is good, he or she will bring both sides to a meeting in the middle so that both are happy.

The Job Offer Acceptance Letter

You've been given an offer, you know about your compensation package, and you are satisfied with it. All that's left is one detail—formally acknowledging that you want the job. This is typically done with a job offer acceptance letter.

If your employer makes an offer over the phone and you accept it, you should follow up immediately with an acceptance letter. This is the expected protocol as well as a courtesy to the company. While your acceptance letter is not a contract, it may be useful should any problems arise over the formal terms of your employment. Send out the job offer acceptance letter to the company via certified mail—so that you know it has been received. And be sure to keep a copy for your own records.

Make sure that your acceptance letter has all the necessary components. First and foremost, you should thank the company for the offer and state clearly that you accept it. You should also include your position title, start date, the details of your compensation package, including benefits, and any other relevant information that you and the company have agreed upon. The tone of the letter should be cheerful, letting your employer know that you are excited about joining the team.

In some cases you won't need to mail your own job offer acceptance letter. For example, your employer may send an offer letter and/or a formal employment contract, negating the need for you to mail a separate document. This scenario occurs frequently, especially if you've met the employer in person to negotiate your salary. In the offer letter or contract, the company will include the particulars of your employment, including your compensation package, and then ask you to sign and return the form. Before signing, read it very carefully (it doesn't hurt to have a knowledgeable friend read it too) and be sure that you understand and agree with all the terms. If you don't, contact the company immediately and ask for clarification. If there are any changes to the details of your employment, ask that another document reflecting these alterations be mailed to you. Sign and return the document only when you are satisfied with it. When it comes to accepting a job, it is your responsibility to know exactly what you are agreeing to.

Even if you don't need to write your own job offer acceptance letter, you might want to send thank-you notes to those who are responsible for hiring you. This is a great way to express your gratitude while starting off your new job on the right note.

Example of a Job Offer Acceptance Letter

Chester Summa
405 Any Avenue
Portland, OR 97204

May 27, 20XX

Linda Adriani
Senior Human Resources Manager
Great Employer, Inc.
100 Great Employer Lane
Suite 500
Portland, OR 97206

Dear Ms. Adriani:

I am very pleased to accept your offer of employment for
the position of Customer Service Representative at Great
Employer, Inc. Per our discussions, I understand that I
will be earning an annual base salary of $28,000, a signing
bonus of $3,000, and standard company benefits. I further
understand that I will receive full pay during the 8-week
customer service training program that commences on June
15, 20XX, my first day of work.

As we agreed, my hours will be from 8:30 a.m. to 5 p.m.,
Monday through Friday, and I will be stationed in the
corporate headquarters in Portland. I am looking forward
to working under the direction of my immediate supervisor,
Ms. Aileen O'Brien.

Ms. Adriani, thank you again for giving me the opportunity
to work at Great Employer, Inc. I look forward to joining
the team and to contributing to the growth of the company.
If there is any other information you need from me in
advance of my start date, please don't hesitate to contact
me at (503) 000-0000.

Best Regards,

(signature)

Chester Summa

Key Chapter Points

◆ In most cases, you can and should negotiate your compensation package with your employer. Companies seldom approach the compensation negotiation process with only one number in mind. They can be flexible if you can positively and persuasively argue why you deserve more.

◆ Find out the typical salary range for the type of job you are being offered, keeping in mind that your location, level of experience, and other factors will influence the outcome. You can determine a practical range by researching salary survey sites and speaking with employees in your industry, especially those employees who hold jobs similar to the one you are considering.

◆ A great way to prepare for compensation negotiation is to practice, much the same way you practiced for your interviews. Ask a friend to play the part of the company representative in a mock negotiation. When the two of you sit down to discuss what you'd like to earn on the job, audiotape or videotape the encounter. When you've finished, replay the tape and see which of your methods of communication were the most effective.

◆ When negotiating compensation, tone is very important. You'll want to sound persuasive, but also flexible and congenial. Hiring managers dislike working with arrogant candidates, so be sure your confidence doesn't border on overconfidence.

◆ During negotiations, you, as the candidate, want the employer to be the first to suggest a base salary, or least a salary range. If you're first, you run the risk of stating a number that is less than what the company would have offered you, or else, stating a number that is higher than the company is wont to give.

Chapter Eleven

OUTWITTING THE JOB MARKET LONG-TERM

You've found a great job, you have every right to celebrate. Go out on the town. Eat a good meal with your friends. Make a toast to your own future. But don't forget that while you've outwitted the job market in the short term, you'll have to keep your eye on the long term too. That's right—outwitting the job market is actually a career-long pursuit. As long as you're in the workplace, you'll have to plot and strategize ways of staying ahead. Fortunately, this isn't as hard as it sounds. The tips below are a good starting point for taking advantage of the opportunities your new job will offer—and creating a few opportunities of your own.

Seven Strategies for Success

UNDERGO REGULAR CAREER SELF-APPRAISALS

You go to the doctor once a year for a complete physical examination; why not undergo an annual career examination too? The self-appraisal is a way to take stock of your continuing career-related achievements and goals. At least once a year, write down a list of the skills and experiences you hope to be gleaning from your job and where you want to be in the coming year. By comparing this list to what is actually happening, you will be able to determine the rate of your professional growth. If your job is helping you to achieve most of your desired career goals, then you know you are making good progress. If, however, there are sizable discrepancies between your "wish list" and your "reality list" over a reasonably long period of time, you may want to consider renewing your job search efforts.

One management consultant says she takes off a personal day every six months specifically for the purpose of self-appraisal. "I usually spend the day outdoors, in a park or hiking. I take my list with me. Away from work and the usual interruptions at home, I'm able to be more objective. I can be honest with myself about where my job is going, where I want to be, and whether those two directions dovetail."

Thinking long-term doesn't hurt, either. Where do you want to be in your career in five years, ten, or twenty? What can you do now to ready yourself for these goals? Considering the distant as well as immediate future can help you to make important decisions regarding your career. Explains a thirty-one-year-old professional who works for a prominent accounting company: "I have a rough idea of where I want to be, using age as a scale. I want to be in a management role by the age of thirty-five, for example. If I'm not there in a few years, I have to assess some things. Why am I not getting promoted? Am I not performing up to the [necessary] level? Or is the company overlooking me because of something beyond my control? [If this is the case,] I'll have to find another company to stay on track." For this employee, as well as for many others, short- and long-term career appraisals are a regular part of work life.

PAY ATTENTION TO YOUR PERFORMANCE REVIEWS

Many employers, especially large corporations, consider job performance reviews a standard part of the cycle. Once every six months, or once a year, your boss—and sometimes your peers and subordinates too—will review your on-the-job performance based on competencies such as leadership, teamwork, and problem-solving abilities. You will be graded, in a sense, the same way you were graded in school.

It's natural to balk at the thought of performance reviews. Yet if you choose to ignore them, you will also be ignoring their impact on your career prospects. Indeed, performance reviews are often weighted heavily when promotion time and raise discussions come around. If you're serious about moving ahead in your field, don't be passive about performance reviews. Tackle them head-on. Be gracious when your strengths are pointed out, but pay more attention to the areas that need improvement. If your supervisor says that your presentation skills are lackluster, for example, make an effort to improve them. Take a public speaking seminar; maybe your company will be willing to subsidize it. There are plenty of ways to improve perceived weaknesses in your employment performance: Read books. Take classes. Enroll in online courses. Seek the advice of those who are adept in the areas that you are trying to shape up and sharpen. In the process, be sure that your supervisor is aware of your attempts at self-improvement. Don't assume that she is in the know and will automatically take into consideration your efforts at your next performance review.

And what about those long months between reviews? Don't wait for your employer to initiate discussions about your job performance. Approach your boss and ask, "Am I working up to your expectations? Do you have any suggestions for how I can become a better employee?" Being proactive about your own improvement is a great way to get noticed for the right reasons.

And speaking of getting noticed—the next time you're praised in an e-mail, letter, or memo, be sure to keep a copy. Keep a folder for the express purpose of collecting items that illustrate your value to the company and your continuing improvement. Keep copies of your performance reviews, too. The next time you begin a job search, this folder will help to convince future employers that you're worth hiring.

STAY ON GOOD TERMS WITH YOUR BOSS

Your boss is the person who will recommend you for a promotion, if the opportunity arises. For this reason and for many others, staying on good terms with her is imperative. Put time and effort into the relationship. Try to think from your boss's perspective. What drives her? How does she do her job? And more importantly, what can you do to make her job easier? If there's an important project in the works, for example, don't hesitate to put in extra hours. Do the bureaucratic tasks that you know your boss detests. Come in early and stay late to make sure you're always available should your boss need you. If you can lighten her workload in a helpful rather than invasive way, you will make yourself more valuable. In fact, if you can become indispensable to your boss, she will bring you up with her if *she* is promoted.

But what can you do if, despite your best efforts, your relationship with your boss isn't working out? One account manager describes his difficult experiences with his former manager. He says, "My boss and I were actually competing for the attentions of *his* supervisor. My boss's boss had taken a liking to me and had even given me some of the important duties that would normally have been my boss's domain. There was some rivalry there, even though I didn't want there to be. I spoke with my boss about improving our relationship. I thought we could meet once a week for a lunch meeting, just the two of us, to sort of mend our working relationship. But he was opposed to all my suggestions—perhaps he felt threatened—and I realized I would probably need to move on." As this example indicates, not every relationship can be saved. If you've been consistently passed over for promotions, if you've been in the same job for a few years despite prospects of upward mobility, if relations between you and your boss are consistently tense or uncomfortable, it may be time to explore other horizons.

If you like your company, one option would be a lateral move. If you take a job at the same level, but with a boss who likes you on a personal level, your chances of promotion will be much greater. Of course, you can also look for employment outside the company.

SPEAK TO THOSE WHO HAVE SUCCEEDED

In your company, or perhaps in your industry in general, you have no doubt encountered people whose work ethic or management style you respect and admire. How did they get to where they are today? What paths did they take? And how do they stay at the top of their game? No matter what level you're at in your company, speak to those people whose abilities, skills, or drive you can learn from. You can do so informally. Sit with them in the company cafeteria. Introduce yourself after a company-wide meeting. Send e-mails asking if you can stop by their offices. Or you can take a more formal approach and ask for brief informational sessions. Either way, by listening to and learning from others, you can cultivate your own professional growth.

By the same token, you may be the person whom others are seeking out. If there are people at your company whom you can encourage and assist, reach out to them. The more friendships you forge, the more benefits—personal and professional—you will reap.

EXCEED EXPECTATIONS

Above and beyond your job description, what else can you be doing to make the most of your position? Complete the tasks expected of you, then strive to do more. An administrative assistant at a nonprofit organization was eager to showcase his technical skills, which he seldom used on the job. When the nonprofit organization decided to replace its outmoded computers, he volunteered to head up a task force to refurbish the old computers and donate them to a local public high school. "Everyone was impressed by my initiative and my sense of giving. I volunteered my time after work because I believed in the cause. But a perk was that my coworkers and superiors noticed that I was really good with technology."

There are many ways to make your mark at work. Volunteer to do something small, like record the minutes of a company meeting. Better yet, tackle a larger problem. Organize a team dedicated to finding a solution for a persistent company problem, or volunteer to complete an unpopular, but high-profile assignment. Consistently go the extra mile, as long as doing so doesn't interfere with your regular workload. Your leadership abilities won't be lost on those around you.

LOOK FOR OPPORTUNITIES BOTH WITHIN YOUR COMPANY AND BEYOND

If you've been in your job for at least a year, a promotion isn't the only path toward career advancement. Applying for and landing an internal job of higher rank and responsibility is another way of getting ahead. Most companies will pick qualified internal candidates over qualified external ones. Beware, however, of applying for an internal position if you haven't spent at least twelve months in your present job. While companies are partial to internal candidates, they don't want someone who will leapfrog from one position to another.

Take a gander at the new openings at your company frequently. Better yet, look for a suitable internal job *before* it's publicized. Sometimes, you'll get a heads-up through word of mouth or office gossip. From there, it's a matter of speaking to the HR person responsible for filling that position.

While applying for an internal position is a perfectly legitimate means of career advancement, don't hide your intentions from your boss. He'll probably find out down the road, through a human resources person or another employee, so you might as well be up-front from the get-go. Also, while it's acceptable to apply for one or two positions, don't apply for every opening under the sun. For one thing, human resources won't take you seriously. And for another, your lack of specificity will signify that you don't have direction. It's much better to wait until the right opening comes.

While looking for opportunities internally is important, don't ignore the opportunities that exist outside of your company. If you successfully used a recruiter in the past, let him know if and when are about to begin another job search. It's also a good idea to keep your résumé available on at least one employment site in case another company wants to contact you about an open position. Just don't make your résumé too available. If you've plastered it all over Monster, HotJobs, and various other job sites, there's a chance your present employer will notice. Getting caught in the act of looking for an outside job is akin to unofficially declaring your decision to leave the company—something you might not be prepared to do.

NEVER STOP NETWORKING

Just because you are happily employed doesn't mean you should halt your networking efforts. In fact, the best time to network is probably when you are comfortably situated in a job. That way, you won't be saddled with the weight of a job search or unemployment. Also, you'll be able to talk freely with your contacts without having to ask them for favors. As mentioned in chapter 3, it's important to communicate with your contacts regularly, not just when you need their advice or assistance.

Keep track of your contacts and how often you communicate with them. It's easy to let months, and even years, pass in between phone calls and e-mails. And the more time that elapses, the harder it is to reestablish contact. Use a calendar, planner, or personal digital assistant to help you organize your correspondence. And don't forget your Rolodex or address book. Keep it updated with the correct phone numbers and e-mail and mailing addresses of each of your contacts.

If you have a long contact list but little time, try to prioritize. Be sure to make time to see in person those contacts who are most important to you. For acquaintances or casual contacts, the occasional e-mail or phone call is an acceptable alternative to a face-to-face meal or coffee break.

While keeping up-to-date with old contacts is crucial to networking, so too is meeting new people. Your new job will mean lots of fresh faces, so don't be shy about introducing yourself. Stop and chat with your new coworkers at company-sponsored parties. Go for drinks or dinner with your department. If your company sponsors an employee sports team or weekend activity that doesn't interfere with more important obligations, sign up.

If your company doesn't offer many opportunities for socializing, invent your own. Ask a few of your coworkers to your house for a dinner party. If time permits, organize a trip to the movies, bowling alley, local watering hole, or a concert. If you want to organize a larger event or to start a club or a sports team, speak to human resources before you forge ahead. You may need the department's consent and to follow a certain protocol. Nevertheless, human resources personnel are thrilled when employees think of new and innovative ways to bolster company morale. Most will be happy to oblige.

Finally, remember that networking will benefit you throughout your career. According to a recent poll conducted by the Society of Human Resources Management and the *Wall Street Journal*'s Career Journal, the percentage of jobseekers who rate networking as an effective job search tactic was 78 percent. Referrals from employees also ranked high at 65 percent. Obviously, when it comes to finding jobs and advancing in your career, the more people you know, the better off you'll be.

Key Chapter Points

✦ At least once a year, undergo a career self-appraisal. Write down a list of the skills and experiences you hope to be gleaning from your job and where you want to be in the coming year. By comparing this list to what you are actually learning on the job, you will be able to determine if your rate of professional growth is satisfactory.

+ Play an active role in your performance reviews. Pay attention to your areas of weakness, be vigilant about improving them, and be sure your supervisor knows about your efforts. If you are up for a promotion, your performance reviews will be weighted heavily in the decision-making process.

+ If you are looking to advance at your company, look for a suitable internal job opening *before* it is publicized. You'll stand a better of getting the job if you express interest in it before other candidates do.

+ Continue to network in your new position. Stay connected with old contacts, but put time and effort into getting to know your new coworkers too. Stop by company-sponsored events and outings. Go for drinks or dinner with your department. Even if your company doesn't offer many social opportunities, make it a point to reach out to those coworkers you'd like to know better.

Chapter Twelve

ON THE ROAD TO YOUR IDEAL JOB: TWISTS, TURNS, AND UNEXPECTED BUMPS

The road to outwitting the job market is riddled with all kinds of twists, turns, and bumps, not to mention detours and roadblocks. Fortunately, there is almost always an alternate route to your desired destination. The following questions and answers should help you on your way.

Q: *My company is downsizing. Should I start looking for a new job before I'm burned too?*

A: Once a company begins downsizing, it is seldom the same—at least in the immediate aftermath. Employee morale may suffer, and the work environment may change significantly. Moreover, one round of layoffs may signal that another is on the way, meaning that existing positions aren't out of the danger zone.

    While you shouldn't assume that you will get "burned," keeping an eye out for other jobs is probably a good idea. Even if another round of layoffs doesn't seem likely, you may decide that switching to a company that is growing rather than shrinking is a sound career decision. You don't have to begin a full-fledged job search, but you can start inquiring about job opportunities within your network. Now is also a good time to update your résumé.

If one round of layoffs has already occurred, you may find yourself doing the work that your laid-off coworkers used to do. This might mean extra hours at the office and less personal time. However, if you question your company's financial stability, it's important that you take time to get your own affairs in order, including undergoing a career self-appraisal (see chapter 11). While company loyalty is admirable, in the twenty-first century no one is immune to downsizing, and you have to consider your own well-being first.

Lastly, remember that finding a job can take months. By sending out feelers now, you'll be getting a head start should you receive that dreaded pink slip.

Q: *I'm an older professional and have had a hard time finding a job since being laid off. I'm angry about the prejudice among companies toward people fifty-five and older. What can I do about it?*

A: There's no getting around the fact that many employers have preconceived notions about older workers and that some of these preconceived notions are negative. In a recent survey published jointly by the Society for Human Resources Management, the National Older Worker Career Center, and the Committee for Economic Development, human resources professionals were asked to cite what they view as the possible disadvantages of hiring older workers. Two of the most frequently indicated disadvantages include "older workers do not keep up with technology" and "older workers are less flexible compared to younger workers." At the same time, human resources professionals cited what they perceive as the benefits of hiring older workers. Two of the most frequently cited advantages include "older workers serve as mentors for workers with less experience" and "older workers have had invaluable experiences in their careers."

While it's a shame that these generalizations exist in the first place, believe it or not, they may actually be to your advantage when looking for a job. Because you know in advance what doubts employers might have, you can address these doubts before they grow. For example, from this survey, you know that many employers fear that older workers are not up-to-date on the latest technology. Here's your chance to prove them wrong. If you are in fact technology-savvy, position this information front and center on your résumé. Make sure it's so visible that employers won't have a reason to use technology as an excuse to pass you over. If you're not technology-savvy, make every effort to be. Enroll in a class or ask a knowledgeable friend or family member to give you regular instruction in whatever area of technology is used in your industry. At the same time, you can play up the positive generalizations that pertain to older workers. You know that many employers assume that older workers can be powerful mentors to younger workers. Reinforce this assumed attribute by stating in your cover letter what mentoring you've done in the past, which will show employers what you can do in the future.

Of course, you can also help yourself by narrowing the scope of your job search. Are you targeting companies that are known for their recruitment and retention of older professionals? If not, why not? The AARP (formerly known as the American Association of Retired Persons), an organization dedicated to addressing the needs and interests of older persons, runs an annual feature in their magazine entitled "The Best Companies for Older Workers." Companies on the 2002 list included CALIBRE, the Aerospace Corporation, Prudential Financial, and the Hartford Financial Services Group, among others. For an updated list, be sure to visit www.aarpmagazine.org.

Another option would be to look for employment organizations and programs that have a vested interest in helping older workers find suitable employment. If you're interested in the environment, for example, one resource you might want to check out is the Senior Environmental Employment (SEE) Program, which places individuals age fifty-five and over in full-time and part-time positions at federal, state, and local environmental agencies (http://www.nowcc.org/applicants/index.html).

Most employers know that the numbers of older persons in the workforce is growing. In fact, according the above survey, the number of workers age fifty-five and over will increase nearly 47 percent between 2001 and 2010, while the number of workers age twenty-five to fifty-four will increase by only 5 percent during this same time period. The fortunate result of these statistics is that employers will need to start looking at older employers in a new light if they want to prosper.

Q: *The company I'm working for doesn't offer as many paid holidays as my last employer. Isn't every employer obligated to offer the same number?*

A: The answer is no. According to the Bureau of Labor Statistics, employers are not obligated under federal law to give paid holiday benefits to their employees. Paid holidays are more or less a perk of any job, and different employers have different approaches to the issue. Most do offer somewhere between four and ten paid days off, but your employer isn't legally obligated to offer any if it doesn't want to.

Q: *What is the right and wrong way to leave a job? I've accepted an offer by another company and am ready to bid adieu to my present employer.*

A: Let's start with the "wrong way" first. What you don't want to do is to announce to your present coworkers in a company-wide meeting that you can't wait to leave. Another "wrong" would be to tell off that one person in your department you never liked. In a nutshell, you want to avoid any dramatic, damaging, or emotional behavior. If your new employer calls your old employer for a reference check, the last thing you want your old employer to say is that you have a bad attitude.

Okay, fine, so what is the right way to say goodbye? It's best to give your resignation verbally, in writing, or both, at least two weeks before your specified date of departure. Most of the time, even if you tell your boss in person of your intent to leave, she will ask you to type up a resignation letter so that the company can have it on record. What should you write? HR experts advise keeping it short and sweet. There's no reason to outline every grievance or pet peeve you had on the job—or how you didn't get the high-profile assignments you wanted. In fact, you should state only that you are resigning and what your last day on the job will be. It's possible that your boss will ask you why you're going. It's a fair question, and should be answered as honestly as you can. Be honest but refrain from making any unduly negative remarks. It's sufficient to say that you learned a lot on the job, were thankful to be a part of the company for the time that you were, but that a new position is the right move for you at this time.

The day of your resignation, there's no predicting how things will turn out. Your boss might plead with you to stay, offering to up your salary or to give you a vacation. Or she might say, "Good-bye and good riddance." All that really matters is that you keep your cool and refrain from saying anything you'll regret later. Remember, in the job market, contacts count—and you want to stay on good terms with all of them. And who knows? Perhaps you'll return to this company again one day.

Lastly, be ready for the possibility of an exit interview. Exit interviews are typically performed by HR personnel in an attempt to understand why employees are leaving. If you're asked to participate in an exit interview, be ready for questions like "Was there anything about your job or this company that you dislike?" and "What kind of support do you wish you could have received while working here?" Again, staying positive should be your priority. Even if you decide to give some constructive criticism, don't present it in a way that will burn bridges.

Q: *I've been laid off. What do I do now?*

A: First, try not to panic. Getting laid off is a blow, but it is something you can overcome. What you'll want to do first is to make sure you can provide for yourself and your dependents. You may be eligible for unemployment benefits, which will help you meet your financial needs in the short term. Since unemployment insurance is administered by individual states, you should check with your local unemployment insurance claims office to inquire about your eligibility, benefit amounts, and the duration of time that benefits would be available to you. The U.S. Department of Labor Website (www.dol.gov) also offers plenty of information on unemployment benefits, as well as links to unemployment insurance sites by state.

When speaking to a person in the claims office, you'll have to have some information on hand, including the name and address of your ex-employer, your salary at your old job, and your dates of employment. Your eligibility for unemployment and your weekly benefits amount will depend on this information.

If you decide to file for unemployment benefits, you should do so immediately after being laid off, since the process is time-sensitive. Moreover, processing your claim can take a couple of weeks, so the sooner you do it, the faster you'll receive your first benefits check.

Bear in mind that unemployment isn't a freebie. It is designed to tide you over while you are actively looking for work. Receiving unemployment benefits may mean you have to report in person to your local unemployment insurance claims office on occasion. Each week, too, you'll likely have to call an unemployment insurance number in order to claim benefits for the previous week. Yet on the whole, unemployment benefits can help assuage the financial burden of being out of work.

Another thing to consider is extending your health care benefits. The Consolidated Omnibus Budget Reconciliation Act, more commonly known as COBRA, was passed in 1986. It enables many who have lost their jobs through layoffs to purchase health insurance at a group rate for a limited time. Medical benefits afforded to most COBRA beneficiaries include prescription drugs, physician visits, and hospital care, among others. In general, COBRA applies to group health plans maintained by employers with at least twenty employees. If you are eligible for COBRA, and choose this option, you will probably be required to pay for your coverage.

The U.S. Department of Labor Website states, "If you are eligible for COBRA coverage, your health plan must give you a notice stating your right to choose to continue coverage under the plan. You will have at least sixty days to choose COBRA coverage or lose all rights to benefits." In other words, don't delay looking into the possibility of COBRA coverage. The sooner you take care of your essential needs, the faster you can start the job search process.

Q: *Help! I think my interviewer asked an illegal question during my interview. What recourse do I have?*

A: You need to be clear on whether the question was indeed illegal. Under federal law, no employer can ask interview questions or base employment decisions on a candidate's sex, race, age, religion, ethnic group, or disability. Some examples of unacceptable queries include "Is Sanchez a Spanish name?" or "Would your religion mean that you can't work on Saturdays?" or "Have you been in the country a long time?" Questions about marital status, childcare, and pregancy are also a no-no.

Unfortunately, such questions do slip into interviews on occasion. It's possible that your interviewer is asking an illegal question out of ignorance and has no intention of using your answer when making a hiring decision. However, since you can't really be sure of your interviewer's rationale, the best thing to do is to understand what's fair and what's not, and to know in advance how to handle an illegal question. You have four options. Probably the best one is to reroute discussion. Rather than answer the question, pick a new topic of discussion—perhaps one of your Key Selling Points—and go from there. Changing the topic will send your interviewer a clear message. If he intentionally asked an illegal question, he will see that you've caught him in the act. If the question was unintentional, he may be grateful to you for tacitly alerting him to his mistake.

A second option would be to state flatly that you won't answer the question. This option is acceptable from a legal standpoint but not ideal, as you will probably appear confrontational in the eyes of your interviewer. A third option is to answer the question. In this case, you should know that by doing so you are putting yourself at risk for not getting an offer. However, if you feel strongly that your answer won't hurt your cause, go for it. Fourth and finally, you can try to strip off the layers of the question in order to get to the core of the issue. For example, if you were asked, "How many children do you have?" your interviewer might really be trying to glean if the care of your children will impact your ability to travel for work or to stay late at the office. If you think you've sniffed out your interviewer's motives, you can try to answer the question as it relates to the position. For example, you might say, "I've always been willing and able to get the job done, even if that requires overtime or travel. My strong work ethic would also apply to this position." While this option can lead to good results, it's not always easy to decode a question successfully—so be careful.

In the end, if you believe your interviewer intentionally asked an illegal question as a basis for making a hiring decision, it's best to seek help. Contact an attorney or the Equal Employment Opportunity Commission immediately. To learn more, visit the EEOC Website (www.eeoc.gov) or call the headquarters in Washington, D.C. at (202) 663-4900.

Q: *I'm thinking of going back to school for my master's degree. But when it comes to my career, I don't know if my investment in my education will pay off. How can I find out if it will?*

A: Unfortunately, there's no sure way to read the future. However, you can get a better sense of the financial value of your degree by doing some research. Would the degree be applicable to your present career—or do you want to get the degree in order to segue into a different line of work? Have you spoken with those who have already earned the degree you are seeking? How have they fared in the workplace?

Of course, the kind of degree you are getting is very significant. A Master of Business Administration (MBA) is arguably more worth more money than a Master of Fine Arts (MFA) in sculpting. (Although naysayers could point to recent article in *Business Week* entitled "The Worst of Times for New MBAs," which spells out how an explosion of new MBA graduates coupled with a dearth of jobs is causing "many students to rethink the goals they had at the start of B-school.") Another thing to consider is if the degree would translate directly into career advancement. In others words, would having this master's degree give you an edge over your competition? Again, you'll have to do some investigating to find out. *U.S. News and World Report* (www.usnews.com) offers annual rankings of graduate schools in many different fields, from Public Affairs to Engineering, and also articles on the long-term value of various programs.

If the degree is something that would benefit you at your current job, it's possible that your employer would be willing to foot at least part of the bill. Check with your human resources department to see if the company offers any kind educational reimbursement program. Some employers, especially large corporations, will pay for one or more classes a year, if those classes are relevant to what an employee is doing on the job. Attending school while working will probably mean taking classes in the evenings and/or on weekends, but educational reimbursement by your employer might be a better alternative than paying the full tuition on your own dime.

Some companies are even willing to pick up the whole tab for more seasoned employees. According to *BusinessWeek*, more than 50 percent of executive MBAs cited that their companies paid their full tuition. The catch for executive MBAs, however, is that most graduates are obligated to return to their employers for a specified number of years after they have finished their degrees.

Ultimately, deciding whether to return to school is a personal choice. While there are many factors to consider before making your decision, take comfort in the fact that education, in general, does indeed pay off. According to a study by the Bureau of Labor Statistics, those with bachelor's degrees make, on average, $17,800 more annually than those with only high school diplomas. Those with master's degrees, in turn, make almost $10,000 more annually than those with bachelor's degrees only. This is heartening news for those who are skittish about hitting the books again.

Q: *I think I've been the victim of discrimination at work. What do I do now?*

A: The first thing to do in such a situation is to ask if discrimination is truly the problem. Seldom does discrimination present itself in a

clear light. Most often it's murky. And sometimes, what you perceive to be discrimination might be something else entirely. Unless
the discrimination is blatant—a racial slur, for example—discuss
your situation with a trusted friend or colleague. Explain the circumstances as objectively as you can and listen to what he or she
has to say. If at this point you still believe that you have been af-
fected by discrimination, you do have options.

The most significant anti-discrimination law covering the workplace is Title VII of the federal Civil Rights Act of 1964. Under Title
VII, workplace discrimination based on race, skin color, religious
orientation, or national origin is illegal and subject to punishment.
The Equal Employment Opportunity Commission (EEOC) en-
forces Title VII, as well as the Age Discrimination in Employment
Act (ADEA) of 1967 and others. There are various forms of restitu-
tion the EEOC can provide under Title VII to those who have been
the victims of discrimination. These forms may include front pay,
back pay, hiring, reinstatement, promotion, and reasonable accommodation, as well as attorney's fees and other associated court costs.

However, moving your dispute to the courtroom may not be
the best way to resolve it. A faster and potentially more satisfying
route is mediation. Mediation involves using an objective third
party to serve as an arbitrator for the two parties in opposition. Although mediation may require a measure of compromise on all
sides, it can lead to more diplomatic and peaceful results. Mediation
is a good option for those who wish to remain in their present jobs
or who want to repair damaged workplace ties. Because it is predi-
cated on cooperation and accommodation, both employer and employee can emerge victorious. If mediation sounds like it might be a
good option for you, ask your human resources department if such
services are offered by your company. You can also learn more
about mediation by communicating with the American Arbitra-
tion Association (www.adr.org/index2.1.jsp) and the National
Association for Community Mediation (www.nafcm.org/).

Last but not least, consider leaving the company in question. While sticking it out may seem like the noble thing to do, there's no reason to stay with an employer that enables or fosters discrimination. The stress you'll be under may take its toll not only on your work performance, but also on your quality of life. Finding another employer, one that is supportive and fair, is a far healthier alternative.

Q: *My husband and I are planning on starting a family. How much time can I take off for maternity leave?*

A: Established in 1993, the Family and Medical Leave Act (FMLA) enables an employee who has met the minimum service requirements (twelve months employed by a company, with 1,250 hours of service) to take up to twelve weeks of unpaid leave for any of the following reasons: the birth and care of a newborn child, the placement of an adopted or foster child, the care of an immediate family member such as a spouse, parent, or child who has a serious health condition, or medical leave if the employee cannot work due to a serious health condition. An employee can take the leave in one block of time, smaller blocks of time as needed, or on a reduced work schedule, such as part-time work for twenty-four weeks.

Not all employees at all companies are eligible for the FMLA, however. One provision is that the person must be employed at a work site with fifty or more employees. This means a person employed by a small business may have to work out her own arrangements with the management.

No matter where you're employed, ask a company representative what policies are in place regarding leave. According to a recent survey by the Society for Human Resources Management, the majority of "respondents stated that their organizations are going above and beyond the provisions of the FMLA." It's possible that your employer is too.

For more information on the FMLA, visit the U.S. Department of Labor website (www.dol.gov).

Q: *I started dating someone at my office. How can I make sure my love life doesn't interfere with my work life?*

A: This is a tricky one. Workplace romances are pretty common, but how individual companies deal with them varies. As discreetly as possible, you should check what your employer's policy is. While workplace dating isn't illegal, some companies are intolerant of office sweethearts, while others take a more liberal stance. Young companies or small companies may not have any policy at all.

Regardless of where your company stands, broadcasting the romance is a bad idea. Think about it—would *you* want to see a couple canoodling in a cubicle? If you haven't already, speak with your new squeeze about the terms of your relationship as they pertain to the workplace. If the two of you share projects, attend the same meetings, or otherwise interact during office hours, you'll want to be cautious about how you behave around one another. It's also important—although not pleasant—to discuss the worst-case scenario: how the two of you would survive in the same office should you break up. The workplace is obviously a bad place for quarrels, bouts of crying, or angry silences, so planning for the worst is probably for the best.

Another reason for frank discussion with your sweetheart: gossip. Interoffice dating is known to generate rumors, and you don't want to give your coworkers reason to talk about you—other than for the great work you're doing. In fact, many office sweethearts choose to camouflage their relationship completely. They worry—rightfully so—that the romance may overshadow or distort perceptions of their work performance.

Perhaps the most important thing to consider is how interoffice dating is affecting you on the job. If your work is suffering as a result of the romance—for example, if your concentration is off or if you're wasting whole hours sending love letters via e-mail—you may have to pull the plug on this relationship or find another job. If on the other hand you're able to separate your work life and your love life, even though the two share the same space, you probably have little to worry about.

Q: *Can my employer penalize me for using my work computer to send e-mails not related to my job?*

A: According to the "2003 E-mail Rules, Policies and Practices Survey," which was conducted by the American Management Association, the ePolicy Institute, and Clearswift, more than 50 percent of U.S. companies monitor their employees' Internet use in some way and enforce e-mail-related policies with discipline or other actions. Moreover, "22 percent of companies have terminated an employee for e-mail infractions." So, yes, your employer can penalize you for sending e-mails not related to your job.

There's no question that the Internet and e-mail use are here to stay, especially in the workplace. According to this same survey, the average respondent spends a quarter of his time at work using e-mail. Over half of the respondents believe that e-mail has made them more efficient. Yet with this surge of use has come a surge of abuse. In response, most companies have written policies regarding e-mail use in the office. Moreover, a high percentage of companies use software to monitor the incoming and outgoing e-mail of their employees. Some companies even monitor internal e-mail between employees.

While sending a couple of personal e-mails throughout your day probably won't land you in hot water, beware of whiling away too much time on the company clock. According to the survey, "[Though] 90 percent of respondents report that they send and/or receive personal e-mail at work, the vast majority say it is under 10 percent of all their e-mail correspondence."

Key Chapter Points

✦ Once a company begins downsizing, employee morale may suffer and the work environment may change significantly. Moreover, one round of layoffs may signal that another is on the way. To ensure your own workplace survival, keep one eye on the overall health of your company and the other on job opportunities offered by other employers.

✦ If you've made a decision to vacate your job, be sure not to sever your ties with your employer. Keep your resignation letter positive and to-the-point. And don't use the exit interview as an opportunity to unleash any pent-up negativity.

✦ Under Title VII of the federal Civil Rights Act of 1964, workplace discrimination based on race, skin color, religious orientation, or national origin is illegal and subject to punishment. If you believe you have been discriminated against for one of these reasons, contact the Equal Employment Opportunity Commission (EEOC) immediately.

✦ Beware of using your work computer to surf the Internet or to send and receive e-mails unrelated to your job. According to the "2003 E-mail Rules, Policies and Practices Survey," more than 50 percent of U.S. companies monitor their employees' Internet use in some way and enforce e-mail–related policies with discipline or other actions.

INDEX